The Executive Medical Services Professional

The Executive Medical Services Professional

What It Takes to Get to the Top!

Donna Goestenkors
Associate Degree
Medical Staff Science, CPMSM, EMSP

Georgia Day
Bachelor of Science in Public Administration

CRC Press is an imprint of the
Taylor & Francis Group, an **informa** business

A PRODUCTIVITY PRESS BOOK

First edition published in 2020
by Routledge/Productivity Press
52 Vanderbilt Avenue, 11th Floor New York, NY 10017
2 Park Square, Milton Park, Abingdon, Oxon OX14 4RN, UK

© 2020 by Taylor & Francis Group, LLC

Routledge/Productivity Press is an imprint of Taylor & Francis Group, an Informa business

No claim to original U.S. Government works

International Standard Book Number-13: 978-1-138-31460-3 (Hardback)
International Standard Book Number-13: 978-1-138-31461-0 (Paperback)
International Standard Book Number-13: 978-0-429-85288-6 (eBook)

This book contains information obtained from authentic and highly regarded sources. Reasonable efforts have been made to publish reliable data and information, but the author and publisher cannot assume responsibility for the validity of all materials or the consequences of their use. The authors and publishers have attempted to trace the copyright holders of all material reproduced in this publication and apologize to copyright holders if permission to publish in this form has not been obtained. If any copyright material has not been acknowledged please write and let us know so we may rectify in any future reprint.

Except as permitted under U.S. Copyright Law, no part of this book may be reprinted, reproduced, transmitted, or utilized in any form by any electronic, mechanical, or other means, now known or hereafter invented, including photocopying, microfilming, and recording, or in any information storage or retrieval system, without written permission from the publishers.

For permission to photocopy or use material electronically from this work, please access www. copyright.com (http://www.copyright.com/) or contact the Copyright Clearance Center, Inc. (CCC), 222 Rosewood Drive, Danvers, MA 01923, 978-750-8400. CCC is a not-for-profit organization that provides licenses and registration for a variety of users. For organizations that have been granted a photocopy license by the CCC, a separate system of payment has been arranged.

Trademark Notice: Product or corporate names may be trademarks or registered trademarks, and are used only for identification and explanation without intent to infringe.

Library of Congress Cataloging-in-Publication Data

Names: Goestenkors, Donna, author. | Day, Georgia, 1946- author.
Title: The executive medical services professional : what it takes to get on top! / Donna Goestenkors, Georgia Day.
Description: Boca Raton : Taylor & Francis, 2020. | Includes bibliographical references and index.
Identifiers: LCCN 2019045965 (print) | LCCN 2019045966 (ebook) | ISBN 9781138314603
(hardback ; alk. paper) | ISBN 9781138314610 (paperback ; alk. paper) |
ISBN 9780429852886 (ebook)
Subjects: MESH: Allied Health Personnel | Leadership | Professional Competence |
Career Mobility
Classification: LCC R697.A4 (print) | LCC R697.A4 (ebook) | NLM W 21.5 |
DDC 610.73/7069–dc23
LC record available at https://lccn.loc.gov/2019045965
LC ebook record available at https://lccn.loc.gov/2019045966

Visit the Taylor & Francis Web site at
http://www.taylorandfrancis.com

"Donna Goestenkors and Georgia Day succinctly capture the ever-changing and challenging role of today's MSP. Newcomers and veterans alike will see leadership through a new lens, while learning strategies to reach your full potential."

Dr. Mary Baker, CPMSM, CPCS, FMSP
Sunbury, OH

"Reading EMSP is like having both champion mentors, Donna and Georgia, on your shoulder. You'll want to keep this book nearby, refer to it often, and recommend it to your colleagues. It's a new resource for the industry."

Larry DeHoyos, CPCS, PESC
Keller, TX

"Reading EMSP is like having an expert whispering in your ear. You'll want to keep it nearby, refer to it often, and recommend it to your colleagues."

Robert Gomes, FACHE
Phoenix, AZ

"Join Georgia and Donna, experts in the industry in navigating the way to take the high road in professionalism and work ethics, but also for insight in the healthcare industry that is still unknown to the average person in Medical Staff Services."

Stephanie Russell, BS, CPMSM, CPCS
Colorado Springs, CO

"To truly excel, an MSP needs self-awareness, ambition, and tenacity. EMSP delivers the roadmap for the climb to the top."

Yesenia Servin, CPMSM
Berwyn, IL

"Donna and Georgia share their 'insiders' perspective on how to succeed in the Medical Staff Services industry. You'll understand how to avoid potential pitfalls, embrace leadership opportunities, take risks and reach your full potential." Don't miss this opportunity to live your dream!"

Nicole Keller, MSHM, CPHQ, CPHIT
Seattle, WA

"In a world where ethics can seem antiquated, Goestenkors and Day stand out from the crowd, championing impeccable principles and standards for Medical Services Professionals. Brava!"

Wendi Stivers, BS
Arroyo Grande, CA

"In the ever changing and chaotic world of healthcare, Goestenkors and Day have hit the mark on the essential tips and tools necessary for career advancement for both the novice and seasoned MSP. A must read!"

Mary Jo Sexton-Tosh, MSA
Swansea, IL

Donna Goestenkors, CPMSM

To My Colleagues

There would be no book without the inspiration each of you has provided me along my career path to learn from, to grow from, to build products and services for, to be motivated by, to push myself toward innovative solutions, to provide rewarding mentorship and to become your loyal and trusted friend. I value you. I respect you. I believe in you.

To My Physician and Administrative Leaders

Physician leaders have been my knowledge and career guideposts from the very beginning of my professional life. They have always believed in my abilities, sometimes even more than I did! I have a wonderful network of lasting relationships with these dedicated healthcare professionals. I will always be an advocate for physicians who provide quality patient care with compassion. I trust you. I admire you. I thank you.

Healthcare administrators at times get a bad rap. However, throughout my career, even when they didn't understand what Medical Staff Services was all about, the administrators trusted that my team and I would build solid systems that were compliant and efficient and processes that were logical and innovative. Your confidence in my skills and ability pushed me to be better. I recognize your efforts. I appreciate your desire to "get it"!

To My Husband, Family and Friends

The support of family and friends is empowering. Many times I have sacrificed attending social events to do the right thing for the employer, the physician, the client, the colleague. You have never complained. You held me with your words of encouragement and let me fly to pursue my dreams and to invest my efforts to accomplish things I never could have imagined. Your confidence in my abilities, knowledge and skills has never wavered – even during times of disappointment. You have been my strength. You have been my constant. You have been the reason. I love you!

Georgia Day, Career Success and Fulfillment Coach

I am so grateful for the many wonderful people who have inspired me over time. My loving husband, Michael, is there for me in every way, day in and day out, our beautiful and talented daughters, Vanessa and Melissa, whose unconditional love make every day brighter, and my sister Barbara, for her unfailing belief in me. Cherished friends, both professional and personal, have sustained me, in both good and bad times; I so appreciate them.

My heart-felt gratitude goes to my clients, who have achieved success in ways that empower and sustain them, and I am fortunate to have been a part of that journey.

Finally, over the past few years, I have been privileged to have coaches, Paris Love, Elizabeth Early Sheehan and Karen Holick, to support and guide me. I so value their intuition, wisdom and encouragement.

Contents

Preface xiii

About the Authors xv

1 What You Don't Know Can Hurt You 1

2 Becoming Your Best Self 9
    2.1   Professional Development Competency Today.......... 9
    2.2   Skills Competence Today 10
    2.3   Impact Of Past And Present On Your
           Future Career 10

3 Getting to the Top – Stretch Yourself 15
    Skills Assessment 15
    3.1   Academic Assessment... 16
    3.2   Workplace Assessment 17
    3.3   Personal Effectiveness Needs Assessment 20

4 Getting to the Top – Adapt and Grow..................... 31
    4.1   Skills/Personal/Career Competence......................... 31
    4.2   Leadership Culture Evaluation................................. 34
    4.3   Organizational Culture.. 38

**5 Getting to the Top – Embrace Your Strengths
   and Weaknesses... 43**

6 Success as You See It 51
    6.1   Customized Competency Model For Industry
           Specialties.. 51

ix

x ■ *Contents*

6.2 Transferrable Skills Between Specialty Areas **54**

7 Generational Shifts in the Workplace **57**
Overview...**57**
7.1 Description Of Generation Types **58**
7.2 Differences And Similarities Of
Generation Types...**58**
7.3 Implications Of Generational Shifts **62**

8 Converging Gender Roles **67**
8.1 Stereotypes...**67**
8.2 Equality..**68**
8.3 Needs And Wants..**70**

9 Rethinking Leadership **75**
9.1 Traditional Vs. Transformational **75**
9.2 Traits And Attributes **77**

10 Emotional Intelligence....................................... **83**
10.1 The New Msp Core Competence...........................**83**
10.2 What The New Core Competence
Skill (EI) Means **89**

11 Good Character – Key to Your Success.................... **93**
11.1 Seek The Truth – It'S All About Ethics....................**94**
11.2 Acting With Integrity – Doing What's
Right Even When No One Is Looking **94**
11.3 Make Effective Decisions **95**
11.4 Demonstrate Moral Strength – Doing
The Right Thing For The Right Reason **95**
11.5 Value Of Character In The Workplace **96**

**12 Facts Versus Perceptions, aka Leadership
Blindness** **101**
12.1 Organizational Culture....................................**101**
12.2 Department Culture **103**
12.3 Team Culture...**105**
12.4 Personal Beliefs..**106**

Contents ■ xi

13 How to Influence Leadership Changes from Within **109**
    13.1   Develop Managerial Effectiveness **110**
    13.2   Inspire Others – Always **111**
    13.3   Develop Teams **111**
    13.4   Leading Teams Through Change **112**
    13.5   Manage The Politics **113**

14 Coaching/Lessons in Leadership **117**
    14.1   Tips From The Field As Shared By Others **117**
    14.2   Practice, Practice, Practice **118**
    14.3   Embracing Your Role **119**

15 Servant Leader **121**
    15.1   Characteristics **122**
    15.2   Approach To Organizational Issues **122**
    15.3   Executive Resources **124**

16 Invest in Your Future **127**
    16.1   Financial **129**
    16.2   Family Collaboration **129**
    16.3   Finding Balance **130**

17 Things to Remember **133**
    17.1   Affirmations – Why They Matter **133**
    17.2   Humor Helps **137**
    17.3   Be A Champion To Others **139**
    17.4   Motivate and Inspire As Only You Can Do **139**

18 Next Steps **141**

Appendix A: EMSP Professional Development Creed **143**

Appendix B: EMSP Code of Conduct **145**

Appendix C: EMSP Core Competency Formula **147**

Appendix D: EMSP Core Competency Model **149**

Appendix E: EMSP Value Assessment Tool **151**

xii ∎ *Contents*

Appendix F: EMSP Core Competency Model – Skills 157

Appendix G: EMSP Core Competency Model – Personal 159

Appendix H: EMSP Core Competency Model – Career 161

Appendix I: EMSP Self-Assessment Competency Tool 163

Appendix J: EMSP Performance Profile 165

Appendix K: EMSP Position Statement 171

Appendix L: Reference Guides 173

Index 175

Preface

What do you need to know to achieve an Executive MSP status (EMSP) – the top of your profession? From a historical perspective, our first book, published in 2012, *The Medical Services Professional Career Guidebook: Charting a Development Plan for Success*, will help you to understand how the Medical Staff Services industry has developed over time. Changes in the industry have occurred dramatically since then. Healthcare is in a state of upheaval and uncertainty, litigation has soared, and reimbursements are declining! You have seen organizations close their doors, mergers and acquisitions accelerate, and drastic changes in technology continue to impact every facet of your jobs. Managing risk and monitoring performance and behavior while using qualitative and quantitative metrics have a direct impact on patient safety.

As leaders today, you face not only operational challenges, but the need for expanded communication skills to maximize the strengths of a multi-generational and multi-cultural work force.

The observations and tips we provide you will help shape the cornerstones of excellence in your leadership roles. With your belief in yourself and the perseverance for which you are so well known, you can make contributions you have only dreamed of and most importantly set the pace for those following.

As consultants, with many years of experience, we have incorporated in this book the principles we use in the educational and coaching programs we deliver. This resource is designed as an industry-first leadership development book and serves as a resource partner to our career development book, *The Medical Services Professional Career Guidebook: Charting a Development Plan for Success*. It will empower EMSPs, as well as other healthcare professionals, to lead with courage, embrace the future, and design a creative pathway giving you both professional and personal satisfaction.

Let's all join in this conversation of excellence and pass along the knowledge across all fields of medicine. Give this book to your colleagues, your boss, your administrator, your physician leaders and associates. Today, become the driving force in shaping the future of the healthcare industry.

Here's to your success!

About the Authors

Donna Goestenkors is a highly successful career veteran in Medical Staff Services, with over 40 years' experience. As a full-time healthcare consultant, speaker, visionary, leader and author, she travels on tour making personal appearances and remotely sharing her expertise, industry knowledge and innovative ideas to solve department and organizational problems and offers solid career advice to master any career challenge.

She is also the co-author of the industry's first career development book, *The Medical Services Professional Career Guidebook: Charting a Development Plan for Success.* It contains precedent-setting career-building information and career roadmap models, a competency formula to measure success, sample position descriptions and recommended resources that must be part of your career portfolio. In addition, Donna and her Credentialing Development Team published another industry-first credential verification compliance and practice guide, "Gold Standard Credentialing", as well as "Gold Standard Recredentialing". Donna is actively connected on professional social media platforms and writes a monthly newsletter, "The MSP Compass", and regularly posts in industry and career-related blogs.

Donna holds an Associate Degree in Medical Staff Science from Kansas City Business College, has achieved the highest industry certification from NAMSS as a Certified Professional in Medical Services Management (CPMSM) and recently

xvi ■ *About the Authors*

completed her course work to achieve the Executive MSP (EMSP) designation. She also has been awarded completion certificates from various leadership and business programs throughout her rewarding career (Business Management, Coaching, Project Management, Career Development, through Stephen Covey/Nightingale-Conant and most recently in Executive Leadership Management through Dale Carnegie).

Donna has served her industry well through volunteer leadership at the local, state and national levels and was elected by her peers in 2005 as the youngest NAMSS President ever to hold their national position. She currently serves as a NAMSS instructor and as Executive Faculty for the Executive MSP Training and Education Program through TMG University.

Donna is an ongoing learner, and has a passion for helping others perform to their greatest potential as healthcare executives. She is an advocate for physician and advanced clinical professional leaders and colleagues from across the United States. She can be reached by visiting her website: teammedglobal.com.

Georgia Day, author, career success and fulfillment coach and speaker, helps professionals in the corporate area get to that next successful step in their careers and those who have forgotten or don't even believe that they can have a life outside of business. She works with them to create practical, workable solutions in both areas of their lives.

Georgia spent time in private industry before developing a career in the public sector. During this time, she served on numerous boards and commissions, both nationally and locally. She and her husband Michael then began their next life chapter, spending 10 years working and traveling full time across the country in an RV with their Irish Wolfhound, settling in Austin, TX. She has served as the President of Kamama LLC since the spring of 2000.

Georgia is the co-author with Donna Goestenkors of *The Medical Services Professional Career Guidebook: Charting a Development Plan for Success*, a ground-breaking educational platform for medical services professionals.

Georgia's latest book, *Female & Fabulous at 40+ – Seven Keys to Your Incredible Future*, designed to give women 40+ tools, guidance and support to learn ways to explore the secret to designing a life that touches their spirit and ignites the flames of hope, is available on Amazon (http://kamama. net/40book). The accompanying 52-week journal is available on her website: www.kamama.net/resources.

Georgia's podcast *Career Success Tips – Words Matter Series* can be found on www.kamama.us.
Her newest program, under development now, is designed to make your performance reviews truly show your value to your organization, but most importantly to you!

Georgia is a Diamond-level contributor to Ezine Articles, an internet-based publishing platform for expert authors around the world. She is an advanced Toastmaster, with certifications in communications and leadership. She received her BS in Public Administration from the University of Texas at Dallas.

Georgia has created a life pursuing her passion for helping people through coaching and still has fun traveling, exploring the world.

Chapter 1

What You Don't Know Can Hurt You

What It Takes to Get to the Top:
Be Aware!

The Medical Staff Services industry is now over 40 years old and has advanced well beyond the verification of credentials and supporting a hospital's Medical Staff. It comes as no surprise to you that healthcare continues to change in significant ways. In many respects, however, the industry, long considered as a beacon to Medical Services Professionals (MSPs), has not met the demands of these changes from a skills competency perspective, as well as properly preparing the MSP for greater success. How, you may ask? They have focused on economics, in part due to federal legislative dictates. Massive insurance changes have forced organizations to combine, slash some services, and rely heavily on new technology to make them competitive and, in some instances, viable. What has been lost in this upheaval is the focus on establishing a structure for employee success. This includes

2 ■ *The Executive Medical Services Professional*

positioning MSPs to advance; to learn the wide variety of options the industry offers. Most lacking, we would assert, is the career path to advance from middle management to senior management and ultimately to the executive or "C" Suite, as an Executive Healthcare Administrator (EHA).

In smaller organizations or those with limited career advancement opportunities, the MSP can strengthen their value by modifying their position description or suggesting position title changes as appropriate. For example, if the MSP frequently interacts with the attorney's office on possible litigation, the risk management office, or the quality section on issues critical to regulatory compliance, improved patient safety, or inter-disciplinary projects, they demonstrate their competence in big-picture thinking. That is, they correctly utilize higher-level judgment, while accepting responsibility for results.

While there are instances of wonderful successes achieved in the industry, sadly, there are more unfortunate stories from colleagues about their dissatisfaction, office unpleasantness, lack of support, few opportunities for development and growth and, frankly, stress-related health concerns. These issues deserve attention. Why do some MSPs succeed and others don't? Why do some MSPs continue to advance while others remain in their entry level positions? Why do some MSPs catch all of the breaks and others can't catch any? Why do some MSPs emanate joy and happiness while others are sur-rounded by negativity and dissatisfaction?

It is because of this dichotomy that a resource book has finally been delivered! MSPs are fabulous about preparing themselves to succeed, but many often lack the needed infor-mation, tools, education, knowledge and mentors to get them on their career development path. In fact, their performance may be labeled as "mediocre" when, in truth, many are high performers and are just like you and me. Those who have been fortunate enough to have a mentoring leader pushing them and coaching them into their next opportunity of success are blessed indeed. With the right kind of guidance, their success stories should far surpass the mediocre workers. In a later chapter, there is a detailed discussion about mentoring that you should find very helpful as you take charge of your career progression.

It is our experience that given the vision, defining the goal, outlining the objectives and having the proper tools, MSPs can accomplish most anything. Successful MSPs understand the importance of collaborating with other stakeholders while enjoying the state of independent thought, work, self-motivation and achievement. There are numerous conversations had with colleagues who express a desire to be given a break, to get a chance, to be supported, to be promoted, to have a job title change, and to be believed in their ability. This guide is the key to converting "wants" to "gets".

This first-of-its-kind resource provides the healthcare professional with a roadmap of how the Medical Staff Services industry is structured, defining the process of identifying individual strengths and developmental areas unique to each environment and competency. We address which core competencies exist within the industry, as well as the soft skills that are required by recruiters and administrators in a highly functioning employee.

There are over 6,000 currently identified MSPs working across the country, serving in diverse work settings, various healthcare and business organizations, and their value continues to expand and grow. Your authors believe that there are literally hundreds more professionals performing the work of MSPs without knowing that they are MSPs and that there is a professional industry just waiting to be tapped into to provide education, resources and support in their career advancement. To optimize professional growth is to understand the foundation of where you are in the field now and to propel you to where you want to be. Millennials are becoming the dominate force within the industry

4 ■ *The Executive Medical Services Professional*

with the Baby Boomers hanging on to fulfill their commitment, because that's what they do! We are very confident that this generation of MSPs will transform the industry as we know it for the better while remaining in greater balance with their career and life responsibilities. Change is happening NOW, and tenure, age and hours worked are no longer the measurement of success. Results and relationships are today's predominate factors of success.

This book describes the impact you can have on the industry, within your organization, department, in your career marketability, advancements and confidence. You will know what to do to get noticed in a good way at work and how to get others interested in your ideas and solutions. This describes a leader. This describes an executive level professional. This describes you – the EMSP.

Getting to the top is not easy, but we have mapped a plan for you that is built on a rock-solid foundation and a time-tested structure that, to the best of our knowledge, NO other industry professional has attempted before. Each chapter you read will help you build on the knowledge, skills and abilities that many of you already have but didn't know how to package yourself or optimize your talent. We will introduce you to the latest proven techniques for success.

One resource tool developed especially for the EMSP is the EMSP Creed, an authoritative list of commitments that the EMSP will follow, which guides their commitment and dedication to their profession. The second foundational resource tool, EMSP Code of Conduct, describes a collection of expected behaviors, principles and beliefs that are fundamental to success. Both have been shared with colleagues across the nation and are available now to you. (See Appendices A and B.)

What You Don't Know Can Hurt You ■ 5

EMSP PROFESSIONAL DEVELOPMENT CREED

I ACCEPT patient safety as my top priority.
I DEMONSTRATE effective leadership.
I DEVELOP and implement an impactful career plan.
I continually PURSUE educational opportunities.
I ACHIEVE mastery in my professional skills.
I COMMIT to self-care so that I can be of service to others.
I EXEMPLIFY competence in all areas of work.
I LEVERAGE technology to increase my productivity.
I FIND creative solutions to difficult problems.
I EMBRACE and drive positive change.
I VALUE cooperation over competition.
I SUPPORT the community of Executive MSPs in learning, growing, and thriving.

EMSP CODE OF CONDUCT

EXECUTIVE MSPs ARE...

- Professionals with integrity
- Relentlessly innovative
- Committed to a safe work environment
- Creative and open-minded
- Willing to ask for guidance
- Proactive in voicing concerns
- Promptly responsive to work issues
- Accountable for mistakes
- Respectful and compassionate
- Actively involved in the EMSP community
- Mentors to others
- Passionate about work and life

6 ■ *The Executive Medical Services Professional*

The world of social media, for example, has changed the landscape of career development forever, as communication modalities and styles now daily impact what you do, and when and how you go about your day. Yet, this one point has greatly affected your relationships with each other, your organizations and the stakeholders you serve. The time savings are beneficial, but the impact that current communications have had on character and integrity must be considered as well.

Adjusting to different employment structures and landscapes as non-traditional work settings are now the norm, as well as working effectively across generational lines. As important as understanding the individual needs of your team, it is vital to have the ability to also navigate the complexities of an organization's culture and political minefields. Both impact your current success and future leadership roles.

Balancing your professional and personal life will continue to be a priority as you move forward with change. Part of the solution to that issue is ensuring that your confidence stipulates your boundaries, that you have developed the tools to assure your skills, abilities and emotional intelligence are the right fit for you and your organization. MSPs are no longer the victims of their circumstance, their bosses or the organization. With change comes evaluation and self-reflection. You can now pinpoint your strengths and make informed decisions about your value in an organization.

My first encounter with MSPs came in late February 2002, when the then Executive Director of the management firm working with NAMSS contacted me to discuss a possible position with the Education Council. I then had an interview with Donna Goestenkors, Chair of that group. I was appointed for a one-year trial as the public member. My first conference call with the group is one I shall never forget – I understood only one word out of ten – you know the medical lingo.

I knew I had to get up to speed quickly and spent many nights becoming familiar with the industry – the good, the bad and the ugly. I count this as one of the best decisions I have ever made! The more I learned, the more respect I gained for a group truly known at that time as an "under-dog". Having experienced many of the pains this group has endured over time, having always been in a male-dominated industry, I had learned how to succeed, many times despite others' wishes.

I am so pleased with the progress this industry has made, both in job progression and recognition. I am so grateful that you put patient safety first! I continue to share, with gratitude, who you are and what you do to everyone I can. Thank you!

Georgia

QUESTIONS AND THOUGHTS TO GUIDE YOU

Why are some MSPs able to navigate the professional world, while others are not? Those succeeding are in control of their careers. What makes a recognized high-performing employee? They search out the necessary information, tools, education, knowledge and mentors.

Next, you will learn why your skills are vital to your ongoing success. Your past professional development, where you are today, and future planning are critical components of the leadership roles you want as an EMSP.

"Success is not final; failure is not fatal; it is the courage to continue that counts."
Winston Churchill

Chapter 2

Becoming Your Best Self

What It Takes to Get to the Top:
Develop Professional Competency

2.1 Professional Development Competency Today

According to *The New American College Dictionary*, published in 1963, skill, when used as a noun, is the ability that comes from knowledge, practice, aptitude, etc. to do something well. This same dictionary defines competence as *adequacy or capacity, sufficiency, etc.* Competency, according to this dictionary, *can be used to describe competence or due qualification or capacity.* This was the general guide used for the next 20 or 30 years. As you will soon learn, these terms have taken on a more clearly applied definition, fitting today's business environment.

You will see these terms used in several ways in this book; the important thing to remember is that, as a professional working toward a higher or more skilled place in the market, you must manage these carefully, thoughtfully and with a deliberate focus on your future.

10 ■ *The Executive Medical Services Professional*

It has never been more important for you to understand your qualifications, to look at what may be missing and why you need to take steps to improve. A quick story will illustrate this for you.

> Recently, an MSP facing a potential promotion realized she did not have all the skills to move her career forward. While her energy, enthusiasm and take-charge attitude served her well, she realized there are skills necessary at the executive level that either she was lacking or needed improvement. Her verbal and written communication skills were not strong, and her executive presence needed help. She took several steps to correct these: she hired a career coach, joined Toastmasters, and sought an outside executive from another industry to help her with her physical presence as an executive. This not only involved how to dress, but what types of activities were done at the executive level and which ones should now be handled by someone else in the organization. These were not ego-driven suggestions; they were designed to help her operate at a different level. She recognizes that these changes take time, patience and periodic feedback from those important to her progress in learning to be an effective executive.

2.2 Skills Competence Today

The emphasis on skills today is vastly different than it was even 10 years ago. An employee's knowledge base, coupled with the flexibility for change and, most recently, emotional intelligence, are integral to your current and future success.

2.3 Impact Of Past and Present on Your Future Career

In the MSP world, positions have changed and evolved with technology and other strong drivers for companies, not the least of which is the bottom line. You have probably seen companies disappear or merge, and many become more international in their focus, at least where personnel are concerned. The face of our work force has changed.

After many years hearing the experiences of MSPs from across the country, one major conclusion, based upon evidence is clear. Healthcare professionals, to succeed, must adapt to change – changes in organization ownership, demographics, culture, departments, personnel, technologies, resources, practices, policies, protocol, etc. An EMSP must be flexible and open to change – often generating the idea and then being the change maker!

Managing change in the workplace, like any successful project, requires a consistent structure and plan that guides, prepares and enables staff to quickly adopt change to achieve excellent results. Change makers and doers will consistently outperform their colleagues. They help staff to remain engaged and motivated while making a positive transition. Communicating often and explaining the WHY of changes are important for implementing successful change management.

Failure to facilitate and drive change results in a decline in job satisfaction and rewarding performance reviews, and misses in project outcomes, which result in decreased self-confidence and increased negative self-talk.

Change in the workplace can inspire enthusiasm or fear, motivation or distraction, collaboration or isolation. MSPs serve in critical positions to ensure that the safety and care of patients are a priority and are the reason many MSPs work so hard to excel in their positions. What MSPs do matters. MSPs are the gatekeepers of patient safety!

So, as you reflect on what you can do differently now to impact your professional future, confront change head-on. Healthcare changes will continue moving faster and faster. Don't stick with the status quo. Change is scarier when you do nothing.

12 ■ *The Executive Medical Services Professional*

Change is inevitable and no business, organization or person is immune. Act and do your best to set yourself up for success.

> As a child, I grew up in a household where the "why" of things was rarely, if ever, discussed. From the very beginning of my career, I vowed to tell someone I was dealing with as much about the "why" as I could. I believe that when people know something about the background of issues they will have to communicate to staff, they can much more effectively operate. This does not mean, however, that everyone will be happy with the instructions they are given.
>
> Unfortunately, in corporate America today, many times the people giving instructions do not understand themselves what they are asking others to do. If you find yourself in this situation, at least ask your boss for some information. Listen, as you may learn more from what they do not say than you will from what they do say. If there is nothing you can elaborate on, you can simply tell your staff that the reasons are confidential and that you will share any future information you can with them, as soon as you can.
>
> Now, I give you a painful experience I had with change. I shall never forget an outside consultant coming to see me about my operation and some changes he saw coming. I was just like an ostrich and refused to believe him. Within five years, the entire operation was outsourced. If I had listened, really listened, and thought about what I could do to minimize the negative impacts to staff of the change coming, all would have been in a better place. I learned a very difficult lesson and have tried not to ever make that mistake again!
>
> Georgia

> **QUESTIONS AND THOUGHTS TO GUIDE YOU**
>
> What does skills competency look like today?
>   Your knowledge base, coupled with the flexibility for change, and emotional intelligence are integral to your current and future success. Do your past and present experiences influence your future career? Yes, they do – with technology and the bottom line financially at the top of the list.

Next, you will see the importance of academic, workplace and personal effectiveness assessments to your overall career success.

"You must expect great things of yourself before
you can do them."
Michael Jordan

Chapter 3

Getting to the Top – Stretch Yourself

What It Takes to Get to The Top:
Flexibility!

Skills Assessment

Professional positions require employees be measured by evaluating core competencies. What does that mean? Core competency is a concept in management theory that can be defined as a group of skills or attributes that employees need to carry out effectively in order to be judged as competent.

Of course, competencies vary between different organizations, industries, departments and positions. You will often find them referenced in position descriptions, provisional employment evaluations and during annual appraisals. At the time of application, interview and upon employment, employees will be required to demonstrate their level of competence for their position of interest.

16 ■ *The Executive Medical Services Professional*

3.1 Academic Assessment

Let's be blunt here. Many organizations are now requiring degrees, many times in specialty areas, for job candidates in supervisory, management and almost always in executive roles. Whether they are looking for degrees emphasizing healthcare, project management, administration or other areas, they are looking for specialized skills. Human Resources departments are scrambling to keep up with industry changes which affect position descriptions and evaluations. Where possible, you should strive to develop a relationship which helps them better understand your roles. Competition has forced leaders to look even more closely at their bottom line and employees are expected to both avoid costs and improve the organization's financials. They do look at grades; however, they are usually more interested in whether a candidate can complete a multi-year project – such as getting a degree.

A recent conversation illustrates this point. A healthcare executive recently shared a story about an applicant she had for a newly changed position in the Medical Staff Services area of the organization. After holding conversations with other executives, she determined that a higher level of responsibility was appropriate for this group. Why? The organization legal issues and increased government rules and regulations meant that higher levels of decision making and judgment would be required. The Human Resources Department created the new position description, with input from appropriate staff, and sent out announcements for the new position. The position would now require a minimum of a bachelor's degree and preferably a masters in the healthcare field. Internal and external candidates were invited to apply.

The internal applicant who had been performing at least part of the advanced responsibilities had credentials and some college work, but no degree. Several outside applicants had degrees, but no experience in the specific area. The healthcare executive hiring the candidate had a difficult choice to make. They could possibly arrange with the internal candidate to get a degree within a specified period. Alternatively, they could hire the

Stretch Yourself ■ **17**

outside candidate, knowing there could, at least initially, be resentment and possible work slowdown until the group got to know the new person and develop trust.

After evaluating all issues, the outside candidate was chosen. During their interview, they had discussed a sophisticated business project involving a small team that had to be successfully completed prior to graduation. They had demonstrated the advanced critical skills necessary from college to move that part of the organization forward in the best way.

It is worth noting that smaller organizations may lack the financial resources to hire candidates with degrees. In this case, they would look for the type and depth of experience as they conduct interviews and hire candidates.

Based upon this real-life selection process described above, it is the recommendation of your authors that the selection of best-fit professionals within your organization be those who possess the needed skills, experience and emotional intelligence for the position. However, due to the shortage of MSPs, when industry experience is non-existent or lacking, selecting professionals who possess strong emotional intelligence skills, are goal oriented, demonstrate a professional presence and have a positive attitude will serve you well. The lack of experience can be overcome with targeted training and mentoring.

3.2 Workplace Assessment

Core competencies fulfill three criteria:

- Affords the professional access to a wide variety of environments (aka "areas of specialty").
- Skills and attributes must make a significant contribution to the benefits of an organization and/or customer.
- These strengths are difficult to imitate by competitors. (Uniqueness counts!)

For the last 15+ years, I have conducted research among leading MSPs, healthcare systems and organizations, non-healthcare related Fortune 500 companies and the US Government to determine how their organizations define employee competence. This competence definition includes how an employee supports and nurtures their organization's culture. Of the 19 different sources queried, the three most prevalent qualities describing competence are:

Knowledge (noun) = Acquaintance with facts, truths or principles, as from study or investigation.
Skill (noun) = Coming from one's knowledge, practice, aptitude; competent excellence in performance.
Ability (noun) = Competence in an activity or occupation because of one's skill, training or other qualifications.

Using these validation sources of competence, Team Med Global Consulting (TMG) created a measurement formula specifically designed for MSPs and EMSPs, which can be easily applied to any professional trade.

Based upon the EMSP Competency Formula model displayed below (see Appendix C), you will recognize what competency

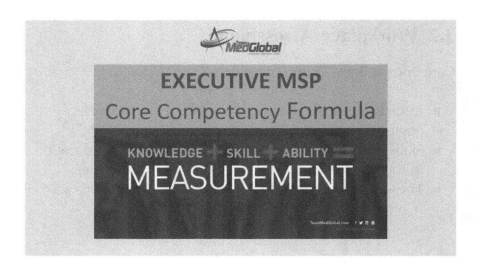

measurements are currently used in the Medical Staff Services industry. This formula has, to date, never required adjustment as it pertains to how an EMSP can measure their competence. This performance equation continues to stand the test of time!

Now that we know **how** we as professionals will be measured. The next important factor to be considered is **what** performance indicators will be measured.

Again, my extensive experience working in the Medical Staff Services industry and serving 18 years as a volunteer leader for our industry's professional organization as well as working as a healthcare consultant has given me many opportunities. I've had the rewarding experience to talk to, work with and create solutions for many.

Each time someone shared a story of success or a situation that didn't have a favorable result and required improvement, I would document these conversations – sometimes very specifically and other times using brief notes. Why, you might ask? These events permitted me to recall the conversation and, as a consultant and life-long learner, to be able to compare, contrast and use this varied information in my client work to achieve even greater results.

The findings from my research and experiences revealed that working successes and failures could be categorized

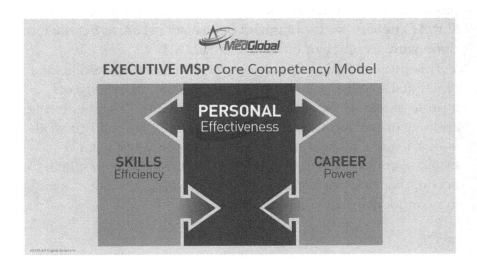

20 ■ *The Executive Medical Services Professional*

into three intra-dependent areas of competence (as noted in the EMSP MSP Core Competency Model, p. 19, and Appendix D).

Skills Efficiency = How efficiently does an EMSP perform their technical trade?

Personal Effectiveness = How effectively does an EMSP demonstrate their professionalism and ability to get along well with others?

Career Power = The result of an EMSP having the ability to demonstrate both technical skills and personal effectiveness skills, including emotional intelligence, thereby creating and generating the most powerful career opportunities!

3.3 Personal Effectiveness Needs Assessment

Seriously, how many colleagues do you know who are very strong in performing specific tasks (SKILLS), but they can't seem to work well with others, in teams, or they always have some kind of drama buzzing around them (PERSONAL)?

Conversely, how many colleagues do we know that have dazzling personalities and know how to "talk the talk" (PERSONAL) but are so disorganized or just can't seem to get the job done with accuracy or efficiently (SKILLS)?

This professional deficiency equates to those soft skills (aka emotional intelligence skills) that impact the relatability of a professional. How well is one able to adapt to change, create and nurture relationships, identify stakeholders, build or work within teams, manage stress, create a home/work balance, facilitate critical conversations, etc.? These skills are essential to ensure that one possesses a sense of well-being while conveying confidence and competence.

Humans have an inherent desire to be liked and to be respected. The truly successful EMSP will have strong technical skills and demonstrate compassion, sensitivity, integrity and good listening skills – the total professional package.

When taking a careful look at yourselves and abilities and assessing how you are doing, you may be limiting your view because you are seeing yourself from your perspective only. Getting feedback from others helps to better understand how others see us. This outreach of perspective often allows for new discoveries about yourself.

Perform the Self-Assessment

Some questions that will aid you in this assessment process might look like these:

1. Who am I as a professional when I am at my best?
2. What keeps me at my best?
3. What do I need to be at my best?
4. What do I consider my top strengths?
5. How do I use these to benefit my work? My team? My organization?
6. Where do I see growth opportunities to use more of my strengths?
7. In what area(s) do I feel there is more opportunities for growth?
8. How would this enhance my work results?
9. Where, in my work, do I feel I could be even more effective?
10. If I were to work on one thing to be more competent and effective, what would it be?

Take some time away from the office and sit quietly as you consider your responses. We suggest handwriting rather than

22 ■ *The Executive Medical Services Professional*

typing your answers as that promotes the head and heart connection and produces deeper and richer results.

Get Feedback

Seek a confidant, an organizational leader whom you trust, a mentor, or an honest colleague to reveal and discuss your answers to these questions. In their critique, ask for specific instances or examples whenever possible that validates their critique of your competence. You need to have a clear picture as to how you are being perceived so you can be more aware and manage yourself more effectively.

When completing this professional development exercise, you will have a rich source of information from which to build upon and strengthen your competence. The goal of this lesson in self-discovery is to use the results as a tool for making or adjusting your targeted learning that will help you function at the level of an EMSP.

I recently found an article written by Steve Pavlina, American self-help author, motivational speaker and entrepreneur. Please note that this information is available in Appendix E, called "Executive MSP – Value Assessment".

These values are also on his website, stevepavlina.com/blog/2004. He has uncopyrighted the information below and I think you may find it helpful as you search for answers. This article lists values which may give you a clearer sense of what is important in your life.

One way to use it is to go through the list yourself and identify the values you feel pertain to you. Another option is to have several close friends, either personal or professional, go through and identify the values they feel pertain to you. I chose both options. Having someone else see you through their eyes is amazing – some values were the same and some were ones I had not seen in myself.

Stretch Yourself ■ **23**

List of Values:

1. Abundance
2. Acceptance
3. Accessibility
4. Accomplishment
5. Accountability
6. Accuracy
7. Achievement
8. Acknowledgement
9. Activeness
10. Adaptability
11. Adoration
12. Adroitness
13. Advancement
14. Adventure
15. Affection
16. Affluence
17. Aggressiveness
18. Agility
19. Alertness
20. Altruism
21. Amazement
22. Ambition
23. Amusement
24. Anticipation
25. Appreciation
26. Approachability
27. Approval
28. Art
29. Articulacy
30. Artistry
31. Assertiveness
32. Assurance
33. Attentiveness
34. Attractiveness
35. Audacity
36. Availability
37. Awareness
38. Awe
39. Balance
40. Beauty
41. Being the best
42. Belonging
43. Benevolence
44. Bliss
45. Boldness
46. Bravery
47. Brilliance
48. Buoyancy
49. Calmness
50. Camaraderie
51. Candor
52. Capability
53. Care
54. Carefulness
55. Celebrity
56. Certainty
57. Challenge
58. Change
59. Charity
60. Charm
61. Chastity
62. Cheerfulness
63. Clarity
64. Cleanliness
65. Clear-mindedness
66. Cleverness
67. Closeness
68. Comfort

24 ■ *The Executive Medical Services Professional*

69. Commitment
70. Community
71. Compassion
72. Competence
73. Competition
74. Completion
75. Composure
76. Concentration
77. Confidence
78. Conformity
79. Congruency
80. Connection
81. Consciousness
82. Conservation
83. Consistency
84. Contentment
85. Continuity
86. Contribution
87. Control
88. Conviction
89. Conviviality
90. Coolness
91. Cooperation
92. Cordiality
93. Correctness
94. Country
95. Courage
96. Courtesy
97. Craftiness
98. Creativity
99. Credibility
100. Cunning
101. Curiosity
102. Daring
103. Decisiveness
104. Decorum

105. Deference
106. Delight
107. Dependability
108. Depth
109. Desire
110. Determination
111. Devotion
112. Devoutness
113. Dexterity
114. Dignity
115. Diligence
116. Direction
117. Directness
118. Discipline
119. Discovery
120. Discretion
121. Diversity
122. Dominance
123. Dreaming
124. Drive
125. Duty
126. Dynamism
127. Eagerness
128. Ease
129. Economy
130. Ecstasy
131. Education
132. Effectiveness
133. Efficiency
134. Elation
135. Elegance
136. Empathy
137. Encouragement
138. Endurance
139. Energy
140. Enjoyment

Stretch Yourself ■ **25**

141. Entertainment
142. Enthusiasm
143. Environmentalism
144. Ethics
145. Euphoria
146. Excellence
147. Excitement
148. Exhilaration
149. Expectancy
150. Expediency
151. Experience
152. Expertise
153. Exploration
154. Expressiveness
155. Extravagance
156. Extroversion
157. Exuberance
158. Fairness
159. Faith
160. Fame
161. Family
162. Fascination
163. Fashion
164. Fearlessness
165. Ferocity
166. Fidelity
167. Fierceness
168. Financial
    independence
169. Firmness
170. Fitness
171. Flexibility
172. Flow
173. Fluency
174. Focus
175. Fortitude

176. Frankness
177. Freedom
178. Friendliness
179. Friendship
180. Frugality
181. Fun
182. Gallantry
183. Generosity
184. Gentility
185. Giving
186. Grace
187. Gratitude
188. Gregariousness
189. Growth
190. Guidance
191. Happiness
192. Harmony
193. Health
194. Heart
195. Helpfulness
196. Heroism
197. Holiness
198. Honesty
199. Honor
200. Hopefulness
201. Hospitality
202. Humility
203. Humor
204. Hygiene
205. Imagination
206. Impact
207. Impartiality
208. Independence
209. Individuality
210. Industry
211. Influence

26 ■ *The Executive Medical Services Professional*

212. Ingenuity
213. Inquisitiveness
214. Insightfulness
215. Inspiration
216. Integrity
217. Intellect
218. Intelligence
219. Intensity
220. Intimacy
221. Intrepidness
222. Introspection
223. Introversion
224. Intuition
225. Intuitiveness
226. Inventiveness
227. Investing
228. Involvement
229. Joy
230. Judiciousness
231. Justice
232. Keenness
233. Kindness
234. Knowledge
235. Leadership
236. Learning
237. Liberation
238. Liberty
239. Lightness
240. Liveliness
241. Logic
242. Longevity
243. Love
244. Loyalty
245. Majesty
246. Making a difference
247. Marriage
248. Mastery
249. Maturity
250. Meaning
251. Meekness
252. Mellowness
253. Meticulousness
254. Mindfulness
255. Modesty
256. Motivation
257. Mysteriousness
258. Nature
259. Neatness
260. Nerve
261. Nonconformity
262. Obedience
263. Open-mindedness
264. Openness
265. Optimism
266. Order
267. Organization
268. Originality
269. Outdoors
270. Outlandishness
271. Outrageousness
272. Partnership
273. Passion
274. Patience
275. Peace
276. Perceptiveness
277. Perfection
278. Perkiness
279. Perseverance
280. Persistence
281. Persuasiveness
282. Philanthropy
283. Piety

Stretch Yourself ■ 27

284. Playfulness
285. Pleasantness
286. Pleasure
287. Poise
288. Polish
289. Popularity
290. Potency
291. Power
292. Practicality
293. Pragmatism
294. Precision
295. Preparedness
296. Presence
297. Pride
298. Privacy
299. Proactivity
300. Professionalism
301. Prosperity
302. Prudence
303. Punctuality
304. Purity
305. Rationality
306. Realism
307. Reason
308. Reasonableness
309. Recognition
310. Recreation
311. Refinement
312. Reflection
313. Relaxation
314. Reliability
315. Relief
316. Religiousness
317. Reputation
318. Resilience
319. Resolution
320. Resolve
321. Resourcefulness
322. Respect
323. Responsibility
324. Rest
325. Restraint
326. Reverence
327. Richness
328. Rigor
329. Sacredness
330. Sacrifice
331. Sagacity
332. Saintliness
333. Sanguinity
334. Satisfaction
335. Science
336. Security
337. Self-control
338. Selflessness
339. Self-reliance
340. Self-respect
341. Sensitivity
342. Sensuality
343. Serenity
344. Service
345. Sexiness
346. Sexuality
347. Sharing
348. Shrewdness
349. Significance
350. Silence
351. Silliness
352. Simplicity
353. Sincerity
354. Skillfulness
355. Solidarity

28 ■ *The Executive Medical Services Professional*

356. Solitude
357. Sophistication
358. Soundness
359. Speed
360. Spirit
361. Spirituality
362. Spontaneity
363. Spunk
364. Stability
365. Status
366. Stealth
367. Stillness
368. Strength
369. Structure
370. Success
371. Support
372. Supremacy
373. Surprise
374. Sympathy
375. Synergy
376. Teaching
377. Teamwork
378. Temperance
379. Thankfulness
380. Thoroughness
381. Thoughtfulness
382. Thrift
383. Tidiness
384. Timeliness
385. Traditionalism
386. Tranquility
387. Transcendence
388. Trust
389. Trustworthiness
390. Truth
391. Understanding
392. Unflappability
393. Uniqueness
394. Unity
395. Usefulness
396. Utility
397. Valor
398. Variety
399. Victory
400. Vigor
401. Virtue
402. Vision
403. Vitality
404. Vivacity
405. Volunteering
406. Warm-heartedness
407. Warmth
408. Watchfulness
409. Wealth
410. Willfulness
411. Willingness
412. Winning
413. Wisdom
414. Wittiness
415. Wonder
416. Worthiness
417. Youthfulness
418. Zeal

Georgia

> ### QUESTIONS AND THOUGHTS TO GUIDE YOU
>
> Have you evaluated your academic career? This is important as many organizations are requiring degrees. Do your skills and demonstrated personal effectiveness match the position you would like to have? These components may well mean the difference between staying with your current job or having the job you really want.

In the next chapter, we will look closely at the core projects MSPs manage and the impact leadership culture has on your career progression.

"What you do today can improve all
your tomorrows."
Ralph Marston

Chapter 4

Getting to the Top – Adapt and Grow

What It Takes to Get to The Top:
Demonstrate Competence

4.1 Skills/Personal/Career Competence

The graphics below depict the core competency areas that the industry (based upon our research) has defined as required knowledge and proficiency points. The beauty of this model is that it can be customized and modified to meet your area of specialty/work environment (i.e. hospital, CVO, MCO, payer enrollment or practice management), scope of work or needed areas of development. Not all of these core competency areas (skills/personal/career) would be required for an EMSP to be successful. Yet, having a working knowledge and/or demonstrated proficiency of these identified areas of competence is important to increase your marketability, confidence and competence. Also see Appendices F, G and H.

What are the core projects EMSPs manage and why is this important? EMSPs must be able to identify their core

31

32 ■ *The Executive Medical Services Professional*

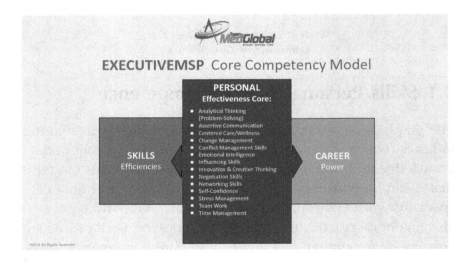

competency areas because management will be evaluating your performance based on them. It also places you in an administrative leadership position because this model, your defined cores, your performance and results will determine your level of executive competence. You are the owner of your work and the results you achieve. Every EMSP must

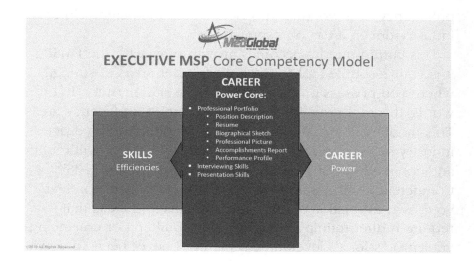

possess knowledge and proficiency, at least in some of these skills, to truly achieve the success and job satisfaction they desire.

Where did this list of core skills come from? Every management function listed is a representation of the industry as obtained through an annual survey and provides benchmarking data and experiences and consists of a core project(s) that EMSPs are responsible for managing in some capacity and in all work environments today. Your work environment/specialty may be slightly different. Again, the tool can be modified by adding or deleting core skills that align with your current position or developmental areas for positions in the future. As our industry and healthcare in general continue to diversify, with organizations merging, selling, buying and, unfortunately, even closing, it is critical for EMSPs to understand how they can measure their competence. This book and this model provide the EMSP with insider information that position EMSPs to be the leaders of change.

Interestingly, this EMSP Core Competency Model continues to expand from its original version of four cores to now a diverse 18 areas listed in the skills set of the core competencies alone. Most contemporary practicing EMSPs must have

34 ■ *The Executive Medical Services Professional*

proficiency or a working knowledge and competence in these industry-driven areas of responsibility.

This current model becomes growth power for the EMSP as it is your resource tool for identifying your areas of strength, where you possess proficiency and have skill mastery. In other words, this tool visually validates your target proficiency areas. This model will also aid the EMSP in pinpointing the exact industry skills, personal skills and career skills that will require additional education, training and practice. Use the EMSP Competency Self-Assessment Tool (Appendix I) to conduct your own evaluation about your strengths and areas that require further training and education. Building or enhancing your professional development plan has never been so easy! Review, select, get busy and produce results.

The goal is to improve your skills, enhance your job performance and increase your confidence in your career readiness. By acting to further your skills toward targeted training and education, it makes you more fully aware of where you are headed professionally and the skills that will require some attention.

We are dedicated to helping EMSPs meet their professional education and career goals.

4.2 Leadership Culture Evaluation

As humans, you are more than just your jobs. You can possess the greatest technical skills in the industry in which to perform your work. However, if you cannot get along with others, if people don't respect your style, or they don't like being around you or don't want you to serve on their team because you are domineering in expressing your point of view or are, frankly, rude and obnoxious, or passive and too quiet, then you will not be considered for a position of greater responsibility.

Conversely, you can have the healthiest and strongest relationships ever known to a professional and you may even be recognized for advancement due to the effective way you manage these relationships. If you do not possess the technical skills required for your position, lead projects, drive efficiencies, get results and work within your budget, you will become the proverbial "grape dying on the vine". The following blunt assessments confirming our work in these areas come directly from organizational leaders. "You will not be respected. Your opinion will not be sought. You will not be the valuable resource you wish to be. You will be considered incompetent. Frankly, you will be likely known as a professional fraud."

Developing competence in both the Personal and Skills categories will serve you well. Your professional presence will complete your profile of competence. This progression of integrating and demonstrating your interpersonal skills and your technical skills will naturally flow into the third category that will drive your career success. This picture of competence you have prepared yourself for will empower you to be considered for positions of advancement and should significantly increase opportunities that empower you to make career choices that will fulfill your dreams.

Let me demonstrate further:

■ Skills Efficiency

These are industry-identified core management functions performed by many MSPs. These functions continue to evolve as demands within the industry and placed upon EMSPs continue to shift and change. A specific example cited pertaining to this described evolution of knowledge and responsibilities required of EMSPs are those core competencies that were identified just 10 years ago.

Over a 10-year time span, the growth and scope of project work for EMSPs changed from four skills core areas to 18 different management and function areas. In this working example, there has been a 350% increase in knowledge expansion, expertise in skills, increase in stakeholder collaboration, a surge in productivity and

36 ■ *The Executive Medical Services Professional*

greater opportunities available for EMSPs. As the evolution continues to define the areas of core competence, the opportunities for ongoing learning and professional development will generate even greater choices and freedom. The future is exciting!

■ **Personal Effectiveness**

Making use of all the resources at your disposal should enable you to master your professional relationships and effectiveness. This group of core competencies are customized to meet your needs, to prepare you for excellence and to aid you in acquiring the ability to act professionally in a variety of situations and with all stakeholders.

Some factors to consider in your pursuit of knowledge regarding your effectiveness are to identify those areas that need a bit of polishing:

- More coordinated workspace
- Enhanced customer service skills
- Increased productivity
- Improved self-confidence
- Effective body language
- Practicing emotional intelligence skills
- Implementing time management techniques
- Managing stress
- Team building skills
- Conflict management skills.

The list of core skills to select from in this competency is limitless. The important thing to know is that any professional development work in this area will be critical in your goal to become an EMSP.

■ **Career Power**

Embracing your career power means you are pursuing opportunities in full readiness, without restriction or barriers of thought; you are in control of your prospects, building your career toolbox, rocking that interview and building your contacts.

Items to include in your career toolbox or professional portfolio:

- Current professional picture
- Current position description
- Current resume
- Current biographical sketch
- Current accomplishments report
- Current performance dashboard.

It's important to remember that each of you wants to be in control of your own future and career path and using this model gives you the power to do so. You own your successes and learn from your failures. Knowing this means it is then logical to believe that being responsible for your own professional and career development is directly linked to your personal effectiveness and the efficiency by which you demonstrate your skills.

Adopting the concept of a measurement formula and competency model and then applying it to your personal work experience will empower every EMSP and healthcare professional to develop a customized career plan. Start today!

What are the steps in beginning to build your plan? We already covered several of them but let's make it simple for you:

1. Conduct a self-assessment.
2. Identify strengths and development areas.
3. Research education and training options.
4. Decide and set career goals.
5. Take action. Work toward your goals.
6. Stay away from negative people.
7. Reach out to stay motivated.
8. Practice positive self-talk.
9. Don't give up.
10. You can do this!

38 ■ *The Executive Medical Services Professional*

This MSP competency formula and model, the career toolbox and preparing for future opportunities is the best plan to be and remain career ready. Through your efforts you should be able to assess, attain and demonstrate your competencies, optimize transferrable skills and be in control of your position decisions.

4.3 Organizational Culture

Organizational culture is described as shared values, beliefs or perceptions held by employees within an organization. Leadership style, decision-making, mutual respect, customer service, quality of service and actions taken in an organization will determine the organizational culture. Some of these same factors will also frame the culture of an industry, a department and the individual. Once established through intent, or lack of attention, culture is very difficult to change. This is an area of consultancy that I am asked about and help develop leadership plans to improve. Behaviors drive culture and equate to job satisfaction.

Organizational leaders must strategically and consciously decide how they and their employees will be expected to interact and behave. It is futile to believe that leaders can establish policies and accountabilities for their employees on issues of importance if they, as leaders, are not willing to or don't demonstrate compliance as well. Every EMSP and employee has the power to influence their own culture, their reputation and others' perception of their competence. In truth, one positive change in behavior can impact the workings of a department. If one person can effect a change in consciousness, just image what a team working toward a unified goal, demonstrating compassion and support toward each other, achieving results to be proud, can accomplish. Culture and quality are infectious. Leaders can positively or negatively impact behaviors and outcomes simply by their use of words,

Adapt and Grow ■ **39**

their work behaviors, their attitudes and their actions. Modeling behaviors for the desired outcome is critical.

The core values of an organization/department begin with its leadership. Employees will be led by these values and the behaviors of leaders. When strong unified behavior and values and beliefs have been developed, a robust and functional culture develops.

Ongoing job satisfaction for staff includes:

- Organizational and department commitment to establishing a desired culture
- Ensuring that the infrastructure supports this commitment
- A clear vision of purpose and expectations for staff.

One of the most powerful results is reduced staff turnover, thereby reducing both human and organizational costs. The power of one is clearly demonstrated. The influence of many is without limit.

Employee satisfaction surveys are conducted as one way to assess employee alignment with organizational/department culture.

Areas surveyed may include:

- Employee orientation
- Customer focus
- Accountability
- Cooperation
- Leader's encouragement and support to subordinates
- Providing clear vision/expectations
- Leader's behavior is consistent with vision
- Communication between leaders and team
- Salary and benefits
- Job satisfaction
- Job recognition.

Organizations who truly respect the results of such surveys will act to ensure employees realize adjustments are being made so

40 ■ *The Executive Medical Services Professional*

they can further their efforts in culture positioning. How many of you have participated in an employee survey and see no demonstrable change from survey time to survey time? That happens all too frequently and will result quickly in a demoralization of the workplace and a slow demise of the organizational/department culture. The solution for your organization or department's failure in this regard cannot be overstated. The value of individual responsibility in creating a culture of excellence through your focused self-development is key. Charting a self-culture mindset of your purpose, vision, behaviors, actions and performance improvement will establish you as a leader. If other leaders around you can't develop or nurture a culture of excellence, compassion and respect, create your own self-culture. As previously illustrated, it only takes one professional to begin changing the work culture. ***Be the one!***

A classic example of an organization's failure to recognize, compensate and support an experienced professional may resonate with you. This professional had been in the industry 20+ years. They had developed and mastered many skills, performed far above their grade level, were respected in the industry and clearly were promotion material. They had innumerable discussions with management about their expectations, and management continued to discount them, refused a title change and any additional compensation. Management clearly did not feel the position or the professional occupying it were of significant value and assumed that, as a long-term employee, they would simply keep going. Wrong assessment – on every level! The employee made sure their professional portfolio was up to date and began interviewing for other positions. They had faith in themselves and their ability to succeed. They landed a job in another state at a significantly higher salary. Yes, this did mean a physical move and certainly family involvement and support. The bottom line here is that now they are happier professionally than they have ever been. Sometimes, making a job change is exactly the right thing to do.

I took the traditional path of going to college right out of high school – a step for which I was emotionally not ready! I played and paid the price for about 20 years. I did get some course work done along the way, but it was only when I turned 40 and asked myself what I had accomplished in life that I realized I was not going to progress at all professionally without a degree. So, while working full time with two teenage daughters, I went back to school for four years at night to accomplish my goal – a bachelor's degree. My husband's support made all the difference, especially when my mother died halfway through the program.

If you do not have the necessary qualifications for the next step in your career, you have some very serious soul-searching to do. You either will take the steps to get what you need, or you will have to become content where you are and be happy with your decision.

Georgia

QUESTIONS AND THOUGHTS TO GUIDE YOU

Looking at the Skills Efficiency core, how many of these apply to you? Do you know how these might impact your evaluations? Why is your professional presence important? Your professional competence in these areas will empower you to be considered for a position of advancement and possible opportunities. Why do you need to understand organizational culture? It impacts every facet of an organization. EMSPs have the power to influence their reputations and others' perception of their competence. Have you participated in an employee satisfaction survey? Were you able to make any changes based on the survey results? Remember that the value of individual responsibility in creating a culture of excellence helps in establishing you as a leader.

42 ■ *The Executive Medical Services Professional*

Next, we will take a close look at the importance of measuring competence to help establish you as a leader in your organization and the industry.

"A clear vision, backed by definite plans, gives you a tremendous feeling of confidence and personal power."
Brian Tracy

Chapter 5

Getting to the Top – Embrace Your Strengths and Weaknesses

What It Takes to Get to the Top:
Recognize Strengths – Acknowledge Weaknesses,
Never Stop Learning

How do you establish yourself as a leader, both in your organization and within the industry? You measure competence and demonstrate your effectiveness in setting a tone of a healthy workplace. This clearly shows your ability to function as an EMSP.

The compatible partner in establishing your professional reputation is your capacity to identify your strengths, areas requiring further development and barriers that prevent you from reaching your goals. As noted in previous chapters, the MSP Competency Formula and associated core competencies are important guides to your future.

What should your first steps be? The MSP Core Competency Model can help. Take a thoughtful look at those listed

44 ■ *The Executive Medical Services Professional*

management functions that you believe you have already mastered. Are there any other aspects of one of these functions that will require just a bit more practice? Be realistic and honest with yourself. You want to be able to speak, perform, explain and/or present on any one of these identified core competencies. This talent is exactly what an EMSP is expected to deliver and deliver with confidence!

Taking a more careful look at the listed management functions within the MSP Core Competency Model, what functional areas will require additional knowledge or training to master or to become proficient to perform or demonstrate? You want to be your organization's resource in any one of these areas that are relevant to your workplace. Look ahead and anticipate decisions your leaders will make that may impact your work. Or, better yet, introduce a new idea or service line that would reduce redundancy, improve processes and enhance customer service. Here are just a few examples of projects where my services were requested on projects by healthcare administrators and professionals just like you. Consider these and recommend one or two of your own. Don't wait for an administrator to request services of a consultant, demonstrate your leadership by proposing projects that will improve your department.

- Determine if the function of payer enrollment can be absorbed by the Medical Staff Services Department.
- Consider recommending the establishment of a System CVO (Credentials Verification Organization).
- Take the lead in performing a needs assessment for purchasing, upgrading or replacing your credentialing or enrollment software.
- Lead the initiative to redesign your department operations.

The point here is that EMSPs must take the lead, be creative, make things happen, drive change and get meaningful results. In order to know where the opportunities exist, you must have a very clear plan of action based upon objective goals and then begin to tackle the required learning and training needed. Once you are confident about your strengths, you can then begin developing a plan to meet your areas of opportunity.

Answering the following questions will help in your plan development:

- What are my target areas of development?
- Are there internal/external resources that can help fill the knowledge gap?
- What financial commitments will prevent me from/allow me to pursue my goals?
- What time commitment will allow me to invest in this professional development?

Do your networking within your local or state organizations and inquire if anyone would be interested in serving as your mentor. If you prefer, there are healthcare consultants, who can also provide you with resources for learning or hands on training.

When thinking about barriers to your success you must consider, in addition to skills and gaps in knowledge, personal growth challenges and career readiness. Personal growth barriers may include being a perfectionist, wanting to perform or be recognized in order to feel valued, being a skeptic or always seeing things as doom and gloom situations, having unrealistic fears, having a lack of support, victimization mentality, being distrustful or cynical as well as time and financial barriers – just to name a few. A professional must be willing to see their fears, change their thinking, act to combat them and then appreciate the positive results that follow. Unfortunately, the negative thoughts we have about ourselves often produce our distorted truth. It doesn't have to be that way. Surround yourself with people who have similar goals, who, like you, work toward self-improvement, are willing to ask for help, confront their fears, take risks and want to perform at their greatest potential, in addition to presenting their most

46 ■ *The Executive Medical Services Professional*

confident selves. With ongoing development, you can turn your barriers into strengths.

Career readiness is another barrier to contend with in advancing your career and when seeking opportunities. However, preparing your career tools is a much easier challenge to conquer. As you have learned in our first career development book, *The Medical Services Professional Career Guidebook – Charting a Development Plan for Success,* the tools you need in your career readiness toolbox are at your fingertips. Here are the career tools that will become a part of your professional portfolio:

- Current position description
- Current professional picture
- Current resume
- Current biographical sketch
- Current accomplishments report
- Current professional performance profile.

The tool that many EMSPs struggle with the most when designing their career portfolio is their professional performance profile. Absolutely everything in healthcare is being measured in some manner. In fact, reimbursements by the government and by health plans are based upon data that reflects the activity and the outcome of care provided by a practitioner. The better their performance, the greater their productivity, the more money they receive.

EMSPs must be their own quality managers, leaders in understanding who they are as professionals, the role they have, the scope of work they cover and the outcomes of the projects they own. Developing and maintaining a professional performance profile or report card of sorts does exactly that. This tool identifies the project, determines the threshold and documents the outcome. All of these data sets will tell the quality story in a snapshot how effective the EMSP has been in managing their projects, how their performance might be improved, where their performance strengths are, all while

Embrace Your Strengths and Weaknesses ■ **47**

continuing to build upon their competencies. This tool is quite remarkable when used and maintained. This can make the difference between an average performance evaluation score or an exemplary score. Think about how this tool can strike the mark of excellence when interviewing for your next position. Give it a try. You will be amazed at the reactions you receive from your superiors as well as how accomplished it makes you feel. We have provided an example of a professional performance profile used by an EMSP (see Appendix J) so that you can use it to begin building your own.

All of the career development tools referenced above are documents that can be maintained in hard copy or in an electronic format and can be labeled, "Career portfolio for [insert your name and credentials]". This tool will become a comprehensive profile that will:

- Reflect your current scope of responsibilities
- Quickly summarize your education, training, experience and talent
- Briefly showcase your achievements and areas of pride
- Reflect the image of your professionalism
- Itemize your project accomplishments
- Report your performance using measurable data.

It is the first impression and final meaningful accessory that people will remember about you. An EMSP Professional Portfolio will get you noticed and will also show management or the potential employer that you are serious about the position and your career. The added benefits of creating an EMSP Professional Portfolio is that you will be reminded about your many accomplishments, you will be encouraged to lead with power and confidence, and you will be confident to present it to others. Finally, it will serve to enhance your competence as a professional because it showcases your awesome talent.

48 ■ *The Executive Medical Services Professional*

In the next chapter, you will learn about the expanded world of healthcare that can broaden your career horizons.

Many years ago, I had the opportunity to apply for a promotion that I knew I was qualified for. I had three days to get the information to Human Resources. I did not have a current resume and frankly did not know how to prepare one. Further, I had no idea how to express and qualify my experience. Because I was unprepared, I did not even get an interview. That taught me a valuable lesson – to become prepared and stay that way. I recognized when my positions became stagnant and took lateral positions twice to get me the experience I needed to progress. Looking at your organization objectively and learning about other areas is critical to your ability to progress. Do your homework and make sure you are prepared.

When I went back to school, I used every minute I could find to study – took my books to the bathroom with me, read at every red light on the way to school after work, read in the bathtub – you get the idea.

How badly do you want to progress? What are you willing to give up to get where you want to go?

Georgia

QUESTIONS AND THOUGHTS TO GUIDE YOU

Do you know how to identify your strengths and developmental issues? Review the MSP Core Competency Model to help you. Is your career readiness up to date? Developing this career portfolio and keeping it up to date may make the difference in a better performance review or job interview.

Next, you will see how you can map your plan for career success, looking at new and different industry specialties, with special emphasis on transferrable skills.

"If you're not willing to learn, no one can help you.
If you are determined to learn, no one can stop you."
Zig Ziglar

Chapter 6

Success as You See It

What It Takes to Get to the Top:
Self-Confidence – Owning Your Role

6.1 Customized Competency Model for Industry Specialties

You have now gained insight into how EMSPs can determine their core areas of competence and those requiring further development. This will allow you to measure your knowledge and proficiency and identify gaps in the areas of skills and interpersonal effectiveness and emotional intelligence when pursuing career success.

It is now time to offer another innovative and industry-setting area for your career development. This is the principle of customizing your scope of core competencies that need to be developed and align them with your specific work environment.

This principle of customization begins first by changing the vernacular in which you refer to your place of work from "environment" to your area of expertise or "specialty". The following are current work environments/service areas where EMSPs

51

52 ■ *The Executive Medical Services Professional*

demonstrate their skills, showcase their talent and practice their expertise. In other words, the EMSP's primary area of specialty:

Recognized EMSP Specialties

- Medical Staff Services Department (MSSD)
- Credentials Verification Organization (CVO)
- Managed Care Organization (MCO)
- Payer Enrollment (PE)
- Practice Management (PM)
- Healthcare Consultant (HC)
- Temporary Staffing (TS)
- Locums Tenens (LT).

These eight major industry specialties provide the workplace identifier for the EMSP. Of course, there are many more, but let's begin with this group of eight. When contacting others within or external to your own specialty, you quickly realize that you may or may not be talking the same language specific to your area of specialty. When you communicate with others about like things, your confidence and your comprehension of topics and your creativity in problem-solving becomes enhanced. When you discuss an industry issue with someone outside of your direct area of specialty, you understand that different words, more information and greater patience will be required to be sure you, as well as your colleagues, understand what is being discussed.

This "area of specialty" principle indicates quickly who has experience in a specific field within the Medical Staff Services industry. Cool, right?!

Well, let's expand this further. Now that you can identify your specialty area, let's enhance that by helping you learn how to create a powerful position statement, also known as an elevator pitch (see Appendix K).

What is a position statement and why is it important? A position statement is a powerful and compelling communication tool that allows you to state succinctly during an

Success as You See It ■ **53**

introduction who you are, what you do and why what you do is important. Your statement should be brief, adjusted according to your audience and delivered with confidence. Practice it often so it just rolls off your tongue.

Here are a few examples of how simply changing how you introduce yourself and including your specialty reference can quickly translate to someone new a powerful, clear and confident message regarding your position. You own it!

- I am an EMSP who specializes in a hospital-based Medical Staff Services Department where we validate the credentials and competence of physicians.
- I am an EMSP who specializes in Payer Enrollment ensuring that providers are paid for their healthcare services.
- I am an EMSP who specializes in CVO operations by confirming the credentials of practitioners.
- I am an Executive MSP with expertise in Practice Management and I manage all administrative patient care aspects in Dr. Smith's practice.
- I am an EMSP who specializes in the placement of temporary clinical staff to be sure we find the right fit and most qualified healthcare professionals for our clients.

I hope you see and hear the difference in how using an effective and proper position statement can make in defining who you are as a professional. It elevates your value, your role and your confidence while increasing how you are perceived by others. Through these examples and the power of words you have the ability to influence yourself and others. Dynamic and commanding power words can make the difference in your success. In these clearly illustrated examples, you convey to your listener who you are, where you work and what you do – powerfully.

This principle has been introduced to MSPs across the country. I am proud to report that I see the power of this principle being used. The action of EMSPs has been demonstrated not only through the use of their position statements

54 ■ *The Executive Medical Services Professional*

but through their behaviors as well. It's truly exciting to experience the confidence in self-awareness beginning to infiltrate the industry in such an empowering way.

6.2 Transferrable Skills Between Specialty Areas

What are transferable skills? Transferable skills are skills and abilities that are relevant and helpful across different specialties, jobs and areas of life – both professionally and personally. Employers frequently look for people who can demonstrate a good set of transferable skills.

Examples of transferrable skills may include:

- Communication
- Dependability
- Teamwork
- Organization
- Adaptability
- Leadership
- Technology management.

Each professional's list of transferrable skills will vary so as EMSPs it will be important for you to express freely examples of your transferable skills, so you remain career ready. This is a fairly new concept in the industry but one that can be quickly mastered.

You learned that transferable skills drive career success. Yet, career success is a subjective term. It can mean something different to you than to me. I personally measure success by the outcome of projects, the knowledge I share, the mutual respect garnered from every relationship, the joy I hope to sprinkle among those with whom I meet and my sense of happiness and wellness at the end of a day.

Won't you take a few minutes to reflect on how you define your personal and career success?

Success as You See It ■ 55

Some of you may be thinking about now, "Gosh, how do I figure this one out?" Here are just a few tips that will get you started on defining your personal definition of what success looks and feels like:

- What are you naturally good at?
  □ Practice becoming the expert!
- Use data to showcase your value (see Appendix J – EMSP Performance Profile)
  □ Data makes your value more compelling.
- Do you make a positive impact wherever you go?
  □ If not, be the change!
- Network and build relationships.
  □ These connections are an investment in your future.
- Describe your self-talk.
  □ Choose to be positive in all circumstances. Practice gratitude.

EMSPs with a clear picture of what success looks like to them will achieve their greatest satisfaction during moments of challenge and will accomplish more goals and build greater self-confidence.

Perhaps the conclusion of this chapter in discovering the lessons learned on your journey to success is to realize that success is living a life to your greatest potential. When you live a life of purpose, you will love what you do because you are making a difference. You will be a person of value, with integrity, living a life toward peace and happiness.

Here's to your success!

Are you able to tell someone in five sentences or less what you do, whom you serve and why? This is especially important if you are talking with someone outside your industry. Do you have a copy of position descriptions for each of the specialties you represent? Notice the aptitudes required in each one. Are there any outside your area of expertise, which you routinely practice, that are not listed in your position description? Learning to use the research method (who, what, when, where, how and why) in widening your horizons is part of your leadership journey.

Georgia

QUESTIONS AND THOUGHTS TO GUIDE YOU

Looking at the customized competency model for industry specialties, do you now know how to customize your core competencies to align them with your specific work environment? Have you thought about your communication skills in relation to other specialty areas? Have you looked at the skills you have or will gain that may transfer to other areas? Why are these things important? In short, so that you will be career ready. You never know when the next opportunity will come; however, it usually occurs when you least expect it – so be ready!

Next, we will look at the dramatic changes in working with multiple generations in the workplace and why you need to understand how to deal effectively with each one.

**"The path to success is to take massive, determined action."
Tony Robbins**

Chapter 7

Generational Shifts in the Workplace

What It Takes to Get to the Top:
Get Along with Others

Overview

The last 25+ years have seen dramatic shifts in similarities and differences in our workforce. In this chapter, we will review research compiled by some well-known marketing firms. Our focus will be Baby Boomers, a sub-set of that generation called Generation Jones, Generation X, Generation Y (Millennials) and Generation Z. We will also look at some generational myths versus realities, affecting the development of employee performance in the workplace.

According to analysts at Pew Research Center, each generation brings a different view of life, culture and ideology, all of whom have been influenced by world events, as well as their national, regional and local history.

58 ■ The Executive Medical Services Professional

What difference does this make in today's workplace, as well as that of the future? What, where, when, how and why work is accomplished has undergone some radical changes over the past 20 years, and your authors believe that will continue to evolve.

So, let's look at the groups, as generally defined by Pew Research and cultural commentator and marketing consultant Jonathan Pontell, to see what leaders today need to understand, as well as future trends that will influence decision-making.

7.1 Description of Generation Types

There is a lot of research describing the prescribed start and end dates of each generation; it can be confusing. To keep it simple, we analyzed the most popular research available and present the most prevalent term dates that describe the current diversity found in today's workforce.

> Baby Boomers = 1942–1953
> Generation Jones = 1954–1965*
> *This is a sub-set of Baby Boomers and was defined by Jonathan Pontell.
> Generation X = 1966–1979
> Generation Y (Millennials) = 1980–1994
> Generation Z = 1995–2015

7.2 Differences and Similarities of Generation Types

Baby Boomers were born just after the end of World War II. Their lifestyles were filled with a save-the-world revolutionary influence. Their early years were very structured and

Generational Shifts in the Workplace ■ 59

conformist, while at the same time experiencing peace, surge in job growth, moves to the suburbs, television, rock 'n' roll music and *Playboy* magazine. They were survivors of the Korean and Vietnam Wars and the beginning of the civil rights movement. The early members of this generation had fairly stable and consistent lifestyles. Women stayed home to raise families and, if in careers outside the home, were typically teachers, nurses or secretaries. Men were in lifetime working positions, with marriage for life, and with divorce and children out of wedlock not acceptable to society. As children, their issues in the classroom were mostly confined to students passing notes and chewing gum in class. As adults, they have maintained an optimistic view of life, are comfortable with team-oriented work and are extremely focused and driven at work.

Those in **Generation Jones** have a shared formative experience between Baby Boomers and Generation X. You will find them at the helm of politics and business. According to Pontell, they now comprise over two-thirds of the current presidents and prime ministers of the European Union (EU) and the North Atlantic Treaty Organization (NATO) member countries. Additionally, they are named both for being anonymous or invisible and for the slang term "Jonesing", an offshoot of "keeping up with the Joneses" that means a craving or strong desire for something. While the Boomers and Jonesers share traits like idealism, they behave differently. Gen Jones members are more practical and rational in their approach to change. Pontell adds their childhood years saw positive social change brought on by the Baby Boomers, but then the sobering events of the 1970s – including Watergate, the oil embargo, rising inflation, and unemployment – forced them to be pragmatic as they became adults. They remember what life was like before the rise of technology, and they want that simplicity. They are willing to unplug from time to time and to use technology as a tool for social betterment and for personal gain and convenience.

60 ■ *The Executive Medical Services Professional*

Pontell comments that those born at the end of the Boomer generation (Generation Jones) broke down societal norms, opting for free love and non-violent protests – which turned into violent events. As adults, they have the reputation of being self-righteous, self-centered and lost the "save for a rainy day" habit, opting for buying now and paying with credit. Women are working outside the home in record numbers, changing the entire nation, as there are now two-income families, where people outside the home began caring for their children. As a group, they are divorcing in larger numbers, and more tolerant of same-sex lifestyles. While some are slow to embrace innovation in technology, they are learning, approaching this and innovation generally as requiring an ongoing learning process. They look at authority in a generally positive way.

One of the biggest changes they bring to American society is their vision of retirement. To them, it means being able to enjoy life after the children leave home. No rocking chairs for them! You are more likely to see them skydiving, exercising and taking up hobbies at a record rate. They are the richest, most free-spending group of retirees in history. They are avid readers with a broad span of personal interest, as well as disciplined, self-sacrificing and cautious. They are comfortable with religion and are generally Christians. It is significant to note that the Baby Boomer generation comprises the largest population of the American worker with Millennials (Generation Y) positioned to surpass the Baby Boomers in year 2020.

Generation X were the first extensive generation of latch-key kids, who came home from school to an empty house as both parents were working. They were raised by the career and money conscious Boomers, watching society's disappointment with governmental authority and the Vietnam War.

Pew analysts described them as being entrepreneurial, very individualistic, and not feeling like a generation, but they are. They are not concerned with government and big business, opting instead for saving their neighborhoods, not the world. One reason for this could be their seeing major institutions

Generational Shifts in the Workplace ■ **61**

failing their parents, or them, while they were growing up. They are focused on making marriage work and to be there for their children. This may have influenced their commitment to self, rather than to an organization or specific career. This generation, according to Pew, averages seven career changes in their lifetime – a far cry from lifetime employment that's usually associated with their counterparts, Baby Boomers.

They want to learn, explore and contribute, while at the same time not valuing loyalty. They are cautious about commitments; their values are relative, and they feel they must tolerate all peoples. They are skeptical, unimpressed with authority, while at the same time self-reliant. Unlike previous generations, they see society and individuals as disposable, tend to divorce frequently, and co-habit before marrying later in life.

The Acquired Immune Deficiency Syndrome (AIDS) epidemic, the Human Immunodeficiency Virus (HIV) and drugs became mainstream and their school problems were far more serious than in previous generations. They became passionate about individual rights, rather than the common good, especially if centered around minority groups. They want what they want and want it now, whether they can afford it or not, and most are deeply in credit card debt.

They have been influenced both by written knowledge and the emergence of digital knowledge, remembering the transition in middle or high school to computers in school. They played video games and watched video movies and embraced newer forms of technology, which may have made face-to-face verbal conversations awkward.

Generation Y/Millennials were nurtured by parents who are very active in their lives and respect authority. They are optimistic and focused and feel like a generation. They feel academic pressure, schedule everything and prefer digital literacy, having not ever been without computers. They get their information and much of their socialization from the internet.

They have seen falling crime rates and falling teen pregnancies. At the same time there are school safety problems and they learned early that the world is not a safe place.

As adults, with unlimited access to information, they tend to be assertive with strong views and prefer to work in teams. They see the world as a 24/7 place and want fast and immediate processing. Unlike previous generations, they have been told they are special, and they expect the world to treat them that way. Many want a more relaxed work environment with a lot of hand holding and accolades and do not live to work.

Generation Z are also known as the i-generation and many in this generation received their first phone when they were 10 years old. They are a hyper-connected generation and using their device is their preferred method of communication. This generation has never known the world to be at peace and they have seen their parents (Generation X) struggle financially. The Zers want to know more about financial education and actually more in this generation open up savings accounts at younger ages.

7.3 Implications of Generational Shifts

Thinking back to the overall stability of the work force of the 1940s to the early 1960s, the generational shifts since then have been significant; some might say radical. Understanding the differences between the generations is critical for leaders to prepare their businesses, their leadership models and adapt recruiting to maximize the benefits to their customers and communities.

Baby Boomers have a save-the-world mentality; Generation X adults want to save their neighborhoods; Generation Y adults have a global perspective for their own personal interests.

Baby Boomers are very focused, structured and conformist, respect authority, working typically for someone else. Generation X adults are entrepreneurial, individualistic and committed to themselves, with little attention paid to government and big business. Generation Y/Millennials are close to their parents, respect authority and are very focused on education, scheduling and digital literacy.

Millennials have a relatively high attention span and focus. However, they are slower than Generation Z to adapt to electronic multi-tasking, using their computers to create and edit documents, research on their phone or tablet, take notes on a notepad, then finish in front of the TV with a laptop, while FaceTiming with a friend. The Millennials tend to be price conscious (remember the recession?). They tend toward higher education, but also venture into working for smaller organizations. Millennials were also the first "global" generation, via the development of the internet.

Effective leaders know the value of clear communication in their organizations. The challenge for today and the future is to create an atmosphere, building on the strengths of diversity among the generations, to achieve the best possible results for everyone. This takes time, patience and practical education to create a harmonious, successful environment.

It is interesting to note that not everyone shares the same opinions about these generations. Let's tackle some generational myths and realities about the generational workforce from another perspective. According to a five-year study conducted by the Hay Group, a global management consulting firm, researchers analyzed data from over 5 million employees across the world. Interestingly, they found that generational differences are more likely attributed to the development of employees, as opposed to their generation. However, general categorizations and traits do carry merit as well, as these attributes aid in initiating discussion which leads to greater insight about us and others. The bottom line of this survey revealed that regardless of an employee's age, they "want the same things". Wow!

Myth #1: Younger Generations Are Less Loyal

All generations described that their most important reason for remaining at their company was to have exciting and challenging work. #Busted

64 ■ *The Executive Medical Services Professional*

Myth #2: Generations Need to Be Managed Differently

The responsibility of keeping team members engaged, regardless of their age, gender or culture, falls on the shoulders of the leader. The leader must adapt their leadership style to meet the needs of each of their team members. #Flexibility

Reality #1: Engagement, Motivation, High Performance

High-performing employees and leaders tap into their emotional intelligence skills – this leads to a greater understanding of individuals and situations.

Reality #2: Important Issues Require Direct Contact

All three generations (Baby Boomers, Xers and Yers) prefer communicating face-to-face for important issues. Their next preferred methods of communication are telephone, email and then text. Feedback from Millennials made it clear that they detest work-related texting.

The characteristics that an EMSP must possess include proficiency in their areas of core competence, emotional intelligence and diversity. They must also demonstrate open-mindedness while promoting a workplace that champions mutual understanding, working toward a common goal, and feeling like they are making a difference for the betterment of others.

> I think dealing with something as complex as this topic means breaking it down into manageable bites. Try putting together an Excel spreadsheet with headers listing employees' names, each generational type, your observations, tasks and projects, and a last one for questions and notes. You may not have the luxury of reassigning anyone to a different task or project! However, based on the information you have put together, you may at least be able to develop a different communication style to gain the support you need to get things done.
>
> Georgia

Generational Shifts in the Workplace ■ 65

QUESTIONS AND THOUGHTS TO GUIDE YOU

To effectively communicate and provide direction to the multi-generational workforce, you will need to develop strategies to fit this new environment. Technology is a significant driver as you move from Baby Boomers to Generation Y. To effectively support your changing executive suite, those you serve, and the industry, you should carefully evaluate both your informal and formal education, including the latest research on the generational cultures. Remember, this will take patience, time and periodic check-ins with the groups to ensure success.

Next, you will see the changing roles for both women and men in the industry, the impacts of increasing litigation and ways to address the relationship needs of MSPs.

"We keep moving forward, opening new doors and trying new things because we're curious, and curiosity keeps leading us down new paths."
Walt Disney

Chapter 8

Converging Gender Roles

What It Takes to Get to the Top:
Discover Others' Strengths, Practice Tolerance and
Give Credit Where It Is Due

8.1 Stereotypes

Over 50 years ago, roles in the workplace were drastically different and very narrowly defined. In the field of medicine, doctors, regardless of specialty, were almost always male. Females in the roles of executives were almost unheard of. Nurses and office staff were considered support roles and were almost always female. Technicians were typically male and even marketing staff from companies selling goods and services to the medical field were male. There were far fewer specialties and record-keeping was at best cumbersome. Frankly, doctors had a narrow frame of reference for the capabilities of men versus women, who were

68 ■ *The Executive Medical Services Professional*

generally expected to be at home raising children and taking care of the mundane but necessary details of life.

The roar of social independence burst forth in America in the 1960s and gender role perceptions began to change. There were an increasing number of women in the workplace, juggling work and home responsibilities, and the social framework shifted. A college education began to be a possibility for women in broadening areas of interest, including the field of medicine.

8.2 Equality

During the 1990s, technology began to reshape the lives of all Americans. The field of medicine exploded with new specialties, with some disappearing and others being combined into new areas of expertise. While insurance companies fought to remain in traditional roles, with limited choices for customers, new vendors introduced creative programs to offer customers a wider variety of services, based on their individual needs. One example of this was the introduction of cafeteria-style health savings accounts, designed to give patients a part in the decision-making process about their family's health needs.

At the same time, women were becoming doctors at an unprecedented rate. The demands of technical professionals with new responsibilities also impacted performance requirements, including additional training, education and in some cases certifications.

While technology was exploding and forever changing the landscape of medicine, along with the number of employed physicians increasing, the crash of 2008 was the final nail in the coffin of "traditional" medicine. Doctors scrambled to find ways to stay afloat, bringing about the large group practices of medical professionals, with the solo practitioner offices greatly reduced in numbers. Added to that were many adults in an aging population with increasing medical issues coming to the forefront.

Women were now entering laboratories, operating rooms and the executive suite. Men were beginning to look at technical and support roles and entering these areas formerly dominated by women. This, just as with other social change, has and will continue to have adjustments in attitudes and approaches to business. Add to this the drastic changes in "traditional" society, where the roles of men and women had been more narrowly defined.

Today, there are more women healthcare executives and leaders than men. Breaking down the prejudices and suspicions so that work can be done effectively takes time and patience and these social lifestyle changes occurred rapidly and openly in the overall scheme of things.

Where does this leave the Medical Services profession? The changes in responsibilities for this group have been astronomical over the past 10 years – those previously thought to be secretaries and administrative assistants – are NOT! Government regulations have mushroomed, legal issues are rampant, technologies are changing almost daily, and quality of service and financial implications have never been more important. Healthcare leaders now rely on specific qualitative and quantitative measures (metric data) to monitor performance across their organizations. Why? Competition in the industry is fierce and organizations now must clearly justify their practices and reimbursement requests. They must determine, for example, whether to keep a doctor on their Medical Staff or panel or decide whether they, or a particular service line, are still effective. These have all had enormous financial impacts to an organization's revenues. The entire face of the medical profession looks different and technology continues to push innovation and dictates when, where and how medicine is practiced.

The "old" view of service provided by MSPs is not only outdated, it has created increased risk. For better or worse, we live in an increasingly litigious society. Insurance companies are in a state of financial crisis. Why? To remain

70 ■ *The Executive Medical Services Professional*

viable and survive, especially with large numbers of organization mergers, they too must be ready to make changes rapidly to compete. The same is true for hospitals as well. Mergers and acquisitions remain an active part of healthcare. The conversion to larger and larger health systems is spurred on by financial crisis, as institutions struggle to stay afloat. At the same time, clinical and other outreach medical facilities are gaining popularity and telemedicine and hospitalist medicine are becoming the norm. MSPs are, at the very least, serious project managers, with the same productivity expectations as more traditional revenue-producing environments. In general, their position descriptions are outdated; there is still little understanding by Healthcare Administrators of the responsibilities MSPs have and that frankly shows in the current hiring process.

8.3 Needs and Wants

So, what can be done to address the relationship needs of this very important group? Position descriptions need to be updated to reflect current responsibilities. Frequent communication – not whining – between the medical services professionals, their peers, their bosses and the patients they serve, must occur. Recognition is critical for a job well done – so those in charge need to ensure this happens. They should be able to quickly analyze performance data, both quantitatively and qualitatively, and recognize positive results. Because the roles these professionals play is so important, vital really to the medical profession, they need to get the training needed and be willing to pay for it themselves if the organization cannot or will not do so. They need to network with groups inside and outside their immediate profession, and take the initiative to improve their technology skills, as well as understanding more about the legal impacts to their organizations. In short, there is no free lunch!

In their roles as project managers, they need to identify how to measure their project results. If they can demonstrate their competence through metrics, their value to their organization is increased in several ways – compliance, competence, improved practices, streamlining technology integration, customer satisfaction, to name a few.

One more point to note is the change in the volume of women in the Medical Staff Services field. Today, more and more men and people of diverse ethnicity are joining the profession. What we see in the industry is a microcosm of what is happening in healthcare in general.

Roles traditionally held are no longer the norm. In the past, hiring practices included those with industry experience first. Now candidates, in addition to demonstrated knowledge and overall competence, have an added dimension. Their expressed value to their teams/organizations includes outreach to professionals without industry experience. Candidates also must possess the proper leadership, emotional intelligence skills, business acumen and overall positive attitude to perform effectively.

An example of gender changes comes from a personal experience early in my career as an EMSP, resulting in an industry-setting decision that influenced the hiring practice in the state of Missouri.

In 1976 I was first hired as an MSP in a growing community in a St. Louis suburb. The population of women physicians on the medical staff of 250 members was 3% (12 women physicians), primarily in the specialties of pediatrics, obstetrics and gynecology. When I left this same community facility almost 29 years later, the landscape was quite different. My facility had expanded to become a main contributor to the BJC Health System. The medical staff had grown to 918 members, with a female population hitting 22% (82 women), which over a 29-year span was an increase of 25%. Women physicians occupied specialty seats in general surgery, neurosurgery, neurology, pathology, emergency medicine, hospitalists, radiology,

72 ■ *The Executive Medical Services Professional*

gastroenterology, colon-rectal surgery along with the more traditional roles in pediatrics, obstetrics and gynecology. Today women physicians are found in every medical specialty.

During my role as a department director, I had the privilege of recruiting, interviewing, hiring and mentoring a number of MSPs new to the field. Some of these professionals have since retired. At one time, at least 10 of my previous team members had advanced to lead and director positions at other metro-east St. Louis healthcare facilities – some at hospitals and others with a system, Credentials Verification Organization (CVO). Additionally, I hired the first female medical staff performance data professional, as well as the first male MSP in the state of Missouri. These three accomplishments highlight the reality of how one person can influence a culture change. Healthcare roles continue to evolve and will continue to adjust to social demands.

Over time, one of the most critical disconnects I hear about is the relationship between the staff of Human Resources (HR) and those involved in Medical Staff Services. In fairness to HR, they are typically understaffed, underpaid, and since they are not revenue-producing, one of the first to experience budget cuts – sounds like the plight of MSPs doesn't it?

I'd like to suggest a few things you may not have pursued to improve this relationship. Many of you in leadership roles perform an invaluable service to new doctors – interns in college etc. participating in workshops, lectures and training workshops. Have you ever thought about inviting someone from HR to join you to hear the dialogue between you and the people you are addressing? How many of you have established a round table involving a variety of stakeholders to look at new ideas and methods you might apply to improve your organization's efficiency and effectiveness? How about asking to cross-train in HR for a day to see how the shoe fits on the other foot? If you want to see change evolve in a way that compliments your objectives, you must find a way to make it happen!

Georgia

QUESTIONS AND THOUGHTS TO GUIDE YOU

Due to the shortage of experienced and trained MSPs, you must evaluate skill sets that are equitable and transferable in placing qualified personnel. To capture the best fit for both personnel and services provided in today's medical environments, the EMSP must understand today's operations and relationships.

Next, you will see the changing roles for today's leaders, with fewer traditional leaders, expanded service lines and a marked increase in transformation and collaborative styles. It is critical to recognize the traits and attributes of each to effectively lead successful organizations.

"Alone we can do so little, together we can do so much."
Helen Keller

Chapter 9

Rethinking Leadership

What It Takes to Get to the Top:
Lead Change

9.1 Traditional vs. Transformational

Traditional leadership typically takes a top down approach.
The President or CEO of an organization is responsible for
the vision, mission, values and goals of the organization.
Have you ever seen a CEO, in place for years, address
a meeting of top management by handing out a written list
of goals for the entire organization to put into place at the
beginning of the new budget year – one month from now?
None of the leaders have seen the material before, much
less have had conversations to see if this could work, given
current staffing levels.

While there are a few organizations who continue this model
today, many have changed their approach to business and
their customers. The changes have occurred over the past 30
years or so, with increased management and employee input
into the organization's direction and culture.

76 ■ *The Executive Medical Services Professional*

What has driven the changes? Fluctuation in the US economy, increased global participation, litigation, competition, customer demands for service changes and employee participation are just a few of the areas marking the need for rethinking what leadership should look like.

Economic pressures impact the structure of organizations and today's leaders have found that some of the best ideas for improvements in methodology, increased efficiency and effectiveness come from within their own organizations. Increased world-wide participation may come in the form of international supplies, techniques and products being used in many parts of an organization. Litigation has played a role in contractual issues, employee satisfaction and the overall delivery of healthcare services. Competition in today's healthcare market is strong and leaders in organizations are very aware of the impact on their operations. Healthcare providers are aware that their customers have choices, so they pay attention to the quality of service delivery. As mentioned in Chapter 7, generational changes have influenced how employees view their positions in companies. Today's employee entering the workplace expects to be included in decisions and wants a collaborative approach to their responsibilities.

So, what does this mean for today's leaders? For those in leadership positions for years, this means they will have or will soon experience a transformational change in their leadership styles and roles. This impacts every facet of their professional lives. They are keenly aware of the need for employee recruitment to meet current standards. This can present challenges as employees may come from different countries and cultures, so assimilation is important. Every level of management needs to understand the ethical, moral, legal and financial responsibilities of the organization.

Today, effective leaders need to be seen, not only in their organizations but in their communities as well.

9.2 Traits and Attributes

What are the traits and attributes of a forward-thinking leader? Recognizing that you will have different personalities, experience, education and styles, you must be willing to take whatever steps are necessary to adapt to today's standards – yet remain true to your values. No one likes a leader who is wishy-washy, indecisive or lacks confidence. Are you a servant leader, learning and growing right along with your employees? Do you have a demonstrated pattern of ethical judgment, effective teamwork patterns and critical thinking skills? Even if you are at a top-level position within your organization and dealing with issues at a much higher level than project management, these skills are very beneficial when analyzing problems and developing solutions.

The traditional role of the MSP has been redefined by the changes in healthcare. As changes go, there are both negative and positive factors that must be considered.

1. The administrative role uniquely of the MSP has been replaced with project management expertise with demonstrated analytical skills with quality metrics. Today's EMSP operates with knowledge of the organization at a much higher level and requires EMSPs to operate strategically.
2. The traditional working MSP was typically found in a hospital's Medical Staff Services Department. Now, you can literally find the high-performing EMSP working in any facet of healthcare. Predominately, you will find EMSPs employed by hospitals but also by CVOs, MCOs, practice management groups, payer enrollment, industry software companies, quality departments, credentialing legal experts, program super users, informatics, locum tenens agencies, and as healthcare consultants. The scope of what an EMSP can do and where they operate is literally boundless, when properly prepared.

78 ■ *The Executive Medical Services Professional*

3. The scope of work performed by EMSPs continues to evolve and requires a broader base of healthcare knowledge, increased proficiency in the expanding specialties within the industry (as reflected on the EMSP Core Competency Model) and advanced technical skills that drive productivity.
4. The isolated MSP, working independently, is a thing of the past. Even if an EMSP is the sole member of a department, they must be able to work in teams, adapt to change, influence change, and work effectively with all stakeholders – both internal and external – toward a common goal.
5. It cannot be over-emphasized that today's successful and highly functioning EMSP must have multi-dimensional knowledge, skills and abilities ranging from content technical skills unique to the industry to relationship management skills that include a keenly developed sense of emotional intelligence that will benefit them in their professional and personal lives. Flexibility, patience and willingness to be a life-long learner are vital to the continued transformation and viability of the industry.

Transformational leadership is a process where leaders and their team members raise each other to higher levels of excellence, morality and motivation. During my long career in this profession I have experienced many situations and have worked in various areas of specialty under numerous job titles. It has been during these experiences in growth that my traditional role as an MSP has advanced to a well-earned position as an EMSP and healthcare consultant. Upon my entry into this profession, experiencing first-hand the lack of available resources and a network to seek assistance, I vowed to work on bridging the existing knowledge gap, to be a guide, and offer insight into industry-specific situations. Being of service

Rethinking Leadership ■ **79**

to others in need hopefully lessens the struggles my colleagues and I experienced.

When I entered this profession, it was shocking to me and my colleagues to discover that there was a woeful lack – meaning none – of available resources to serve as job aids. In the beginning, all we had was each other! This realization moved me in such a way that I made a vow to myself right then and there. I committed that, for the remainder of my career, I would make and seize every opportunity to help my colleagues by bridging their knowledge gap so they could perform at their highest level, thereby advancing the industry. I continue to stand firm in this commitment by taking time to offer support to a colleague in need, by actively working with over 35 colleagues to create innovative education and training resources through books, webcasts, classroom teachings, the industry's first online education platform, podcasts, articles, blogs and social media outreach. In addition, this commitment extends globally by collaborating with clients – some outside of the US proper – vendors and others by taking risks in solving some of our industry's greatest challenges. The industry still has a long way to go to provide fingertip resources for colleagues and healthcare professionals that cover all areas of specialty. However, through the work of many professionals, just like you, more and more progress is being made.

In my travels I am delighted to see the growth, maturity and advancement within our profession. Many EMSP colleagues from across the country participate in professional social groups, are connected through LinkedIn or Facebook and are willing to help others. Sadly, some of our colleagues are not; they are in the minority. More work needs to be done to create an even broader sharing and supporting network. There indeed is power in numbers. Regardless if we are industry Presidents, Vice Presidents, Directors, Managers, Coordinators or Specialists, our mission must be to support one another, champion each other's achievements, coach to improve and promote for success. This mission defines transformational leadership. These efforts

80 ■ *The Executive Medical Services Professional*

describe what successful EMSPs demonstrate and they must remain core to our profession. As human beings and professionals it is our duty to continue to elevate the profession while remaining compassionate, resolute in our commitment of excellence and dedicated in our mission to ensure that quality patient care is delivered ONLY as a result of our efforts of competence.

Leading teams with generational and cultural differences is one of your most challenging responsibilities in my opinion. Assimilation to your organization's roles takes time, patience and increased knowledge – all of this when you already feel somewhat like an octopus! This is where your outside networking can really pay off. If there are not others in your organization who can give you suggestions, email, call or text your friends in other organizations. You do not have to mention any confidential information – simply give a general scenario and listen carefully to their ideas. When dealing with someone from another country, see if you can have a quiet dialogue to see what they might share. This means doing your homework, adding to your knowledge by performing an internet search to see what additional tips you may find.

Georgia

QUESTIONS AND THOUGHTS TO GUIDE YOU

Today's most effective leaders look at their organizations and their communities in a holistic way. They practice servant leadership, operating with ethical judgment and sensitivity. Why is this important? Your adaptability may well mean the difference between your success or failure in the communities you serve.

Next, you will learn about a vital soft skill in your professional development – emotional intelligence. You will see how the four components – self-awareness, self-management, social awareness and relationship management – strengthen your leadership abilities.

> *"It's only after you've stepped outside your comfort zone that you begin to change, grow, and transform."*
> *Roy T. Bennett*

Chapter 10

Emotional Intelligence

What It Takes to Get to the Top:
Be Respectful and Demonstrate Compassion

10.1 The New MSP Core Competence

Yes, the soft skill of emotional intelligence (EI) is the new MSP core competence. Why? Because relationship management is essential in ensuring that EMSPs gain both personal and professional success. More and more clinical professionals are indicating the need to recruit workers who already possess some level of EI skills. In addition, there is an increase in businesses, including healthcare organizations, that are requiring targeted training to further develop the EI skills of employees. Research on this topic revealed that people who possess strong EI skills will be more successful in their position and when interacting with others. EI skills provide the worker with a keen sense of why they react as they do in certain situations, and shows greater compassion and understanding in accepting the behaviors of those with whom they interact.

You, as a developing healthcare leader (EMSP), know well the challenging situations presented by interpersonal issues

83

84 ■ *The Executive Medical Services Professional*

such as misunderstanding of words and intent, others' lack of ability to see the impact of their actions on others, especially relating to patient and family anxiety, diagnosis and treatment, and regulatory complexity. Knowing what to say – effectively communicating your message – is only part of the skill set. You must also know that your behavior and words have an impact on others as well as on yourself.

Healthcare professionals recognize how vital it is to effectively communicate with their stakeholders on a variety of topics and in different settings. Effective communication skills are fundamental to success in many aspects of life. Communication, as you know, is a two-way process, so improving communication involves both how we send and receive messages.

Understanding that there is a difference between communication skills and EI skills will help you improve your professionalism while enhancing the way you manage your relationships.

Communication is a core leadership skill indeed and there is a correlation with your ability to effectively communicate and your ability to lead. Daniel Goleman, who revolutionized the thinking about leadership, describes EI as "the capacity for recognizing our own feelings and those of others, for motivating ourselves, and for managing emotions well in ourselves and our relationships". So, EI can be considered another dimension that must be mastered within the realm of communication and your leadership skills.

Both skills (communication and EI) are important soft leadership skills. Communication is the ability to communicate (speaking as well as listening), while EI is the ability to work with different types of individuals who communicate in different ways.

EI has four compelling attributes:

- Self-Awareness
- Self-Management
- Social Awareness
- Relationship Management.

Emotional Intelligence ■ **85**

Collectively, these attributes give you the tools to know, understand and manage your emotions. Professionals with strong EI have the ability to quickly overcome stress, read social cues, understand what triggers them emotionally, and therefore can maintain their composure. This information should be useful in your ability to drive change, influence others and remain calm and empathic when interacting with others.

You probably have encountered situations like the ones described below:

> A disruptive physician briskly walks into the Medical Staff Services Department without acknowledging anyone upon entry and aggressively asks for the Director. Rather than the Director greeting this physician with care and compassion, he immediately remarks, "Excuse me Dr. X, we don't enter an office in this manner. If you need something, you go back out the door and re-enter the office in a professional way." While this Director perhaps was right in setting the expected tone for his department and protecting his team, we contend that this exchange lacked EI. Why? He immediately redirects on what he expects before first attempting to discover the need of the physician. Did the physician (although disruptive in many circumstances) just experience the death of a patient? Did she recently learn about a critical diagnosis of a family member? Is she going to lose her practice due to poor financial management? Did she just get sued?

Let's look at another example regarding the lack of self-awareness.

> An organization's CEO schedules a team meeting of all directors over the 4th of July weekend. The meeting was held regardless of the personal commitments previously made by those in attendance. The

86 ■ *The Executive Medical Services Professional*

outcome of the meeting was nothing that couldn't have been handled the following week.

Hello! This is America and we celebrate Independence Day! EI is nowhere in sight!

Just these two examples illustrate the negative impact professionals who lack EI skills can have on an organization, department and each other. Unfortunately, these situations happen every day. EMSPs are the leaders in relationship management so let's be the role models.

Now, let's explore the four components of EI more closely.

Self-Awareness

The theory of self-awareness was first identified in 1972 by psychologists Shelley Duval and Robert Wicklund (*A Theory of Objective Self Awareness*, Academic Press). They conducted research and studied the human psyche and its correlation to human behavior. It is their position on the topic of self-awareness that individuals who are in tune with themselves, their behaviors and their values will be better able to control their reactions during difficult and challenging circumstances. So, self-awareness is a major tool in self-control.

However, two psychologists, John Mayer and Peter Salovey, offered the first formulation of the concept of emotional intelligence (EI). This is an even broader concept than the theory of self-awareness. Their research validated the importance of self-awareness and includes not only the ability to understand our self but to actually control and manage our thoughts, emotions and behaviors.

Research has proven that self-awareness is a skill that all successful business leaders possess. EMSPs must practice self-awareness skills to be in the present rather than functioning on automatic pilot.

Your ability to become more self-aware is a skill that can be practiced, tested and sharpened. Self-awareness skills can be nurtured by practicing some or all of these:

- Spend time with your thoughts and truly connect with yourself. Reflect on conversations, experiences and observations held.
- Remain in the present to foster mindfulness. Pay attention on purpose, in the present and non-judgmentally.
- Keep a journal. Record your inner thoughts and feelings.
- Practice active listening skills. Pay attention to other people's emotions and body language and demonstrate empathy.
- Ask for feedback. Don't be afraid to ask others what they think of you. Discern mean-spirited from constructive and genuine.

Self-Management

This is a basic management concept about performing as well as you can and taking responsibility for your own actions. Possessing this skill as part of EI means that you can organize yourself and offer your ideas. It is also about making a choice to do more than you need to do. That is a skill many EMSPs across the country possess.

The three components of self-management are self-explanatory and so critical as practicing professionals:

- Takes initiative
- Highly organized
- Accepts accountability.

Social Awareness

Gives you the ability to understand and respond to the needs of others, thereby improving your social skills and gaining the respect of others. The question to ask yourself is what another

88 ■ *The Executive Medical Services Professional*

person wants and needs and then carefully considering how to meet their needs.

Research reported in *Scientific American* suggests that our levels of empathy (the ability to understand the feelings of others) are lower today than 30 years ago (Lydia Denworth, "The Good and Bad of Empathy", *Scientific American*, December 2017). Why? Perhaps an increase in social isolation due to disruptive technology by way of our devices and digital communication. Understand that when there is no empathy, there is a significant loss of trust.

Again, according to Daniel Goleman, the competencies associated with social awareness are empathy, organizational awareness and customer service.

Relationship Management

This fourth pillar of EI is an initiative that maintains a continuous level of engagement with your key stakeholders both internally and externally through relationship building and ongoing communication. Individuals want to feel that someone is responsive to their needs, seeks their input and values their contributions. These skills promote practices and behaviors that result in a positive and productive relationship.

Competencies related to relationship management include attributes such as influence, leadership, communication, conflict management, teamwork and collaboration.

Here is an example to illustrate this.

> Your boss micromanages EVERYTHING and expects projects and tasks be managed the way she would manage them, versus another approach accomplishing the same outcome. This boss is not only a poor leader but one who doesn't possess EI skills. She lacks confidence, compassion and sensitivity regarding the needs of others.

Emotional Intelligence ■ **89**

Here is another example on a more serious level:

> A team member lingers outside another colleague's
> office, where a conversation begins with another collea-
> gue about the meeting that just occurred. Rather than
> continuing to walk by the office, this employee hangs
> around outside the door to hear what was being said. He
> then goes to the President to spill the beans on the
> conversation. Absolutely no EI was evident in this situa-
> tion! A professional would have continued to walk by
> the door and mind his own business. Or, they might
> have approached one of the two people involved in the
> conversation to ask questions, gain perspective and
> better understand their opinions. That didn't occur! In
> fact, an act of betrayal, judgement and spinelessness did.
> This type of unprofessional behavior will NOT get you
> promoted or respected. EI skills require understanding,
> as well as empathetic and direct communication.

After reading more about the value of EI in achieving successful relationships – both professionally and personally – you are
well on your way to becoming the EMSP and the highest
functioning human being that you desire. Possessing EI skills
as part of your leadership talent will give you a business
advantage that many of your colleagues will be lacking.

10.2 What the New Core Competence Skill (EI) Means

Being skilled in EI allows professionals to seek information
and exchange ideas with others in a way that garners
a high return in value. The successful interaction will build
confidence for the EMSP. Here is an example of what not
to do:

90 ■ *The Executive Medical Services Professional*

> An Administrator who has a rule that no cell phone
> activity is permitted during meetings; yet he is work-
> ing on his iPad processing messages throughout the
> meeting. This "leader" does not possess EI because if
> he did, there would have been a realization that
> corporate rules must apply to all.

MSPs have natural curiosity anyway, but becoming proficient
in this skill will have them seeking out information and
learning about themselves more than other people. They
will do this to validate their direction in order to meet
their goals. MSPs desire project clarity. EI allows them to
avoid distractions and remain focused on the project at
hand.

High performing EMSPs who possess strong EI skills will be
able to take a jammed packed day of planned meetings,
projects and email processing and transition smoothly into
unplanned activities and events, thereby increasing their productivity. EMSPs recharge themselves throughout the day
because they can maximize their interactions with positive
outcomes using EI.

Another benefit to EMSPs of being high performers in EI is
that they know and tell themselves why they need to succeed
on a project. They understand the implications, the impact to
the stakeholders involved and the importance to themselves
when performing with excellence.

EMSPs with strong EI skills are quality performers as well.
Quality output matters to them. They aren't afraid about
knowledge or skill gaps that are currently present in their skill
sets. They are, in fact, tuned in to what they need to develop to
meet and exceed the expectation.

Demonstrating EI skills will serve you and the people you
are interacting with well. With consistency in practice, EI
sensitive people will guide others how to think because when

Emotional Intelligence ■ 91

they impact someone's thoughts or challenge them to grow in a positive way, they have influence.

EMSPs with strong EI skills understand the importance of speaking up for themselves. They share their truth more than other people do. With practice comes proficiency and that develops confidence.

EI allows one to take risks, confront the unknown and discard unwarranted judgments. EMSPs have talent and persistence. Adding the knowledge of EI to their leadership skills will advance their opportunities for success while achieving their greatest sense of contentment.

> What if you are dealing with someone who does not give you any verbal clues in response to a business discussion? I turn to Tonya Reiman, body language expert, whose book, *The Power of Body Language*, is next on my list to read. I have watched her on TV evaluating a variety of people and she seems to hit the mark every time. There are other experts out there – the point is to get help when and where you need it.
>
> Georgia

QUESTIONS AND THOUGHTS TO GUIDE YOU

Emotional intelligence is a critical component of effective relationship management. Why? You want and need effective and positive outcomes in your leadership roles. Practicing interactions using self-awareness, self-management and social awareness will become a cornerstone of successful leadership.

Next, you will look at character traits EMSPs must practice consistently to maximize the best traits of effective leadership – character and integrity. These two traits separate you

92 ■ *The Executive Medical Services Professional*

as a great leader, both thoughtful and courageous in the face of frequent opposition.

"I've learned that people will forget what you said, people will forget what you did, but people will never forget how you made them feel."
Maya Angelou

Chapter 11

Good Character – Key to Your Success

What It Takes to Get to the Top:
Demonstrate Character

Roget's II The New Thesaurus describes **character** as "The combination of emotional, intellectual, and moral qualities that distinguishes an individual".

Roget defines integrity as "moral or ethical strength; the quality of being honest; the condition of being free from defects or flaws, and the state of being entirely whole".

How does this trait impact an EMSP? We have touched on many of the elements in previous chapters, either directly or indirectly. To refresh, some of the character traits necessary for a successful career include:

- integrity, honesty, loyalty, respectfulness, responsibility, humility, compassion, fairness, forgiveness, authenticity, courageousness, generosity, perseverance, politeness, kindness, optimism, reliability, conscientiousness and self-discipline.

94 ■ *The Executive Medical Services Professional*

In this chapter, we will focus on honesty, integrity and the impacts on effective decision-making and moral strength.

11.1 Seek the Truth – It's All About Ethics

Ethical conduct means simply being guided by the principles of good conduct. Part of professional and personal respect is having others know you tell the truth, to the best of your ability. This builds trust in relationships. You can probably visualize someone whom you would describe as "being a person who will lie when the truth will do better". You can also probably think of someone you know who will tell you the truth even when it hurts. In today's workplace, this can be a slippery slope, depending on the organization's culture. However, you are the one who will face yourself in the mirror and see either the truth or lies.

11.2 Acting with Integrity – Doing What's Right Even When No One Is Looking

This kind of decision-making separates the great from the good. It can take courage, perseverance and conviction to assume this as a habit, a part of your daily routine. When you are tired, frustrated and longing to just go home and put your feet up, it can be tempting to take a short cut in a project just to get something finished. Then you re-think your decision and take the time to do what's right. Could you get by otherwise? Sometimes you could, but you are the cream of the crop as an EMSP. You know and will act according to the higher standards.

11.3 Make Effective Decisions

You know that experience, learning from the best in the business, formal and informal education, and learning to quickly analyze the who, what, when, where, how and why are integral to your successful decision-making. There are times when it is best to let a decision lie dormant for a bit (suspecting that it does not need to be made at all). There are other times when the decision impacts a large group of people and the answers are not immediately clear-cut. You learn to balance the needs of the organization with the needs of your groups, wherever possible. The people who report to you and the others who are impacted by your decisions will form a bond of trust and respect because you considered the impact on them. As an EMSP, you give credit to those who helped you in the decision-making process and do not hesitate to apologize if a decision, even made with the best of intentions, is a bad one.

11.4 Demonstrate Moral Strength – Doing the Right Thing for the Right Reason

You can see from the previous sections that moral strength is composed of several traits. For some, this was taught by example at home, in the community or by someone in your life that simply did the right thing for the right reason. If you did not grow up with that kind of example, you can learn how to operate that way. There are a number of educational resources, many of which are free, that you can tap into and you can find people to talk to who can give you sound guidance. No one is perfect. Yet you, as an EMSP, are there to set the pace. Simply remember that when the going gets tough, the tough get going!

96 ■ *The Executive Medical Services Professional*

11.5 Value of Character in the Workplace

The importance of character in the workplace cannot be overstated. Character is essential in attracting and maintaining healthy and positive relationships. It sets the EMSP apart from others. It establishes the tone of who you are, what others can expect from you and garners respect that can sometimes be hard-earned.

When interviewing and hiring a new employee, EMSPs seek out those candidates who have integrity and can provide examples of what that means to them and how their integrity will complement the department's culture.

There's an old saying to "hire on character and develop skills". This philosophy has NEVER let me down when I interview others for industry positions. Character can indeed be shaped and nurtured but it is much easier to educate and train on professional and relationship-building skills.

Shaping one's character is influenced by many factors such as your home environment, your friends, your colleagues, and life's experiences. Think about a situation or a relationship you experienced that revealed to you what you would repeat when given the chance or changes you would make. Your successes and failures in life not only influence your behaviors, your thoughts and your decisions but really define who you are and empower you to be the professional you choose to be.

Many organizations have developed core values that help align an employee's actions with the values of the organization. It is vitally important that EMSPs set the example and make decisions that follow these expectations. This can be practiced by demonstrating respect, coaching and mentoring others when necessary and promoting teamwork to accomplish goals.

Internal and external stakeholders, as well as the EMSP, will benefit by understanding who you are and what you are willing to say and do by the character you consistently display. How others receive you and perceive your character creates

Good Character – Key to Your Success ■ **97**

your reputation. It goes with you wherever you go! Being sensitive to your character makes you self-aware and better able to build and maintain healthy relationships.

Understand that character is the essence of your traits – positive or negative. When your character is put to the test and your integrity is compromised due to a decision you made, words spoken or actions taken, the result will be a direct impact on your reputation – fact! Once your character, especially your integrity, is compromised, it is difficult to regain your footing without doubt or suspicion. Your recovery is time-sensitive and can be more quickly achieved by acknowledging an error, learning from the error and being consistent and persistent in your behaviors, actions and words.

Don't give up. Remember, reputations are recoverable. You must ask yourself, "Is this important to me?" You are the architect of your life. Build it your way.

Here's a true story from a long-time MSP to illustrate these points. The experience she had was frightening, tense and could have had a drastic impact on her career. It really reveals the lessons learned in this chapter about the importance of character, most especially integrity. It all came down to what she was willing to do to please her boss, to be part of the administrative team, to not be looked upon as someone who is not a team player, to wanting to be liked, to being able to have a direct impact on the bottom line.

She was asked by her Medical Director if a reapplication from a specific physician was received. Her response, yes. He then explained that Administration had recently secured the services of a competing specialty group and asked her to "conveniently lose the said physician's reapplication".

She, listening intently to his rationale, acknowledged his comments with appropriate body language and verbalization cues as he continued. After he finished explaining why it was important that this physician's reappointment expire, she responded: "I understand what you are asking me to do. Because you are my boss and the Medical Director, I will do as

98 ■ *The Executive Medical Services Professional*

you ask and will conclude this action by submitting a letter of resignation."

Needless to say, the Medical Director dropped the subject and no derogatory action against the said physician's reapplication was taken. He was reappointed without restriction – the appropriate decision.

An important note to make about this experience is that this colleague had to decide immediately how she was going to manage this request. She was aware that her decision was putting her career and job at risk. However, she was confident in her decision because she knew she was doing the right thing. An unexpected bonus from her decision was that the Chief of Staff learned of this during his weekly meeting with the Medical Director. The Chief of Staff brought her into the Medical Staff Leaders meeting and they all thanked this EMSP for acting in the best interest of the Medical Staff – like a true executive.

This experience points out that EMSPs must always strive to do the right thing. EMSPs make difficult executive decisions every day that potentially could compromise their integrity. It is this type of decision-making that separates the high performer from the average MSP.

I am sure you have been placed in awkward situations just as I have over time. One of the most awkward for me was when I had a great deal of confidential information I could not share – and people knew that I knew. I tried more techniques than I can frankly recount. However, I finally came up with wording from which I would not deviate, "I do not have an opinion about that", and repeated it until they gave up.

When dealing with ethical situations and being given "loaded" questions, if possible, I asked for time to think about what had been said. If someone in top management insisted on an answer, I would at least ask clarifying and

Good Character – Key to Your Success ■ **99**

confirming questions, sometimes asking how someone important outside the organization might react to the decision. While I came close several times, I did not have to put my job on the line. I did however begin to quietly look for other opportunities.

Georgia

QUESTIONS AND THOUGHTS TO GUIDE YOU

Do you fully understand how ethics and trust impact good conduct? Can you recall a situation where you have made a difficult yet appropriate decision? Adding moral strength to ethical conduct will clearly set you apart when making important decisions.

Next, you will learn how easily perceptions can differ from reality and lead to leadership blindness.

"Circumstances are beyond human control, but our conduct is in our own power."Benjamin Disraeli

Chapter 12

Facts Versus Perceptions, aka Leadership Blindness

What It Takes to Get to the Top:
Serve as a Role Model

12.1 Organizational Culture

According to Gotham Culture (https://gothamculture.com/), the term "organizational culture is defined as the underlying beliefs, assumptions, values and ways of interacting that contribute to the unique social and psychological environment of an organization" (David Needle, 2004, *Business in Context: An Introduction to Business and Its Environment*, Cengage Learning EMEA). The culture of an organization will also guide the behaviors considered acceptable: Norms, language, communication style and modality, restrictions, prejudice, attire, body art and piercings, work hours, commitments, accountabilities etc. Simply stated, culture means the way things are done.

101

102 ■ *The Executive Medical Services Professional*

The core of culture focuses on what shapes habits, behavior and repeated behaviors.

Organizational culture can be nebulous when leaders fail to identify expectations or communicate these expectations clearly with staff. It is the responsibility of an organization's highest leaders to create, communicate, practice and evolve the workplace culture. Culture is a continuous process of change (learning and developing) and organizations must adjust in response to internal and external forces.

When effective leaders demonstrate alignment with culture, it promotes greater employee performance. They are able to accomplish their goals based on stated expectations. This results in higher job satisfaction and more honest employee feedback. Cultural awareness is a critical element in an organization's success.

Organizations that have not clearly defined their culture and expectations or are inconsistent in complying with the rules that support a specified culture may result in dysfunctional or toxic work environments. These types of workplace environments can negatively impact employee morale, performance and productivity, damage the reputation of an organization, increase the legal risks due to policy non-compliance and result in costly inefficiencies.

Another factor that must be considered when determining the important role an EMSP holds within an organization is leadership blindness. This type of myopic thinking or a failure to consider different perspectives prevents growth in an organization and limits their leadership in adapting to needed changes, receiving new ideas or making improvements based upon feedback from staff and key stakeholders.

When a new leader enters an organization, they must clearly articulate their vision of what they want to achieve during their tenure or term. They will obviously look at how the organization operates and how goals will be achieved. Yet, the blending of new ideas into the healthy aspects of the existing culture

Facts Versus Perceptions, aka Leadership Blindness ■ **103**

will usually result in less disruption, early acceptance of change and overall support that will lead to success.

An emotionally intelligent and effective leader understands that executives who engage early and establish a positive vibe as they go about their daily work are creating a healthy workplace for themselves as well as their staff. However, when the example set is not positive, is disrespectful or lacks compassion, it can result in friction and frustration.

Here is a reminder of an example mentioned in an earlier chapter that further illustrates the importance of an organization's culture and how non-compliance destroys respect and trust. The culture in this organization restricted the use of cell phones during all meetings. However, the very person who instituted this rule, the hospital's CEO, was also the person who habitually abused the rule. The message to the employees: Different rules for different people!

12.2 Department Culture

The goal of every strong leader is to create a departmental culture that provides your team members with an empowering, respectful and productive workplace.

As already outlined, clear communication with team members about vision and expectations is critical to ensure that a strong foundation is established in setting the tone of department practices and relationship management. Culture can be like a person's personality. A department has expectations, beliefs, interests, experiences, assumptions and habits – just like a human being. These types of traits create the essence of a department's culture; a culture that is shared by a team of people from written, spoken or unspoken "rules" in working together. We "get it" on how to proceed even without a written guideline.

EMSPs have the power to influence a department's culture. It is about:

104 ■ *The Executive Medical Services Professional*

1. Checking your professional habits/behaviors
   a. Are you habitually late to work?
   b. Are you out of the office frequently running personal errands?
   c. Do you meet budget goals?
   d. Are project deadlines missed?
   e. Do you overreact in situations?

2. Learning what is acceptable and not acceptable when interacting with other team members
   a. Are you polite?
   b. Do you refrain from the use of profanity?
   c. Do you actively listen?
   d. Do you gossip about other colleagues?

3. People shaping the culture
   a. Are you shy or outgoing?
   b. Do you have an open- or closed-door policy?
   c. Are you possessive or do you freely share your knowledge and documents?
   d. Do you exhibit positive or negative energy?
   e. Do you accept differences within a team?

4. Creating quality work products
   a. Do you hold yourself and others accountable?
   b. Do you encourage free thinking?
   c. Do you champion ownership?
   d. Do you audit your work?

5. Embracing change
   a. Do you communicate change requests clearly and reinforce expected outcomes often?
   b. Do you involve the appropriate stakeholders?
   c. Do you offer education and training to learn new practices?
   d. Are you compassionate, understanding and kind during the change cycle?

Happy employees are those that feel the greatest connection to their purpose and can then contribute to the larger organizational goal. The culture of a department determines how and why things get done. It is the engine within an organization. Success in performance, productivity and retention are outcomes of high-performing departmental cultures. Are you positively impacting your department's culture?

12.3 Team Culture

According to writer Alana Brajdic, team culture means the values, beliefs, attitudes and behaviors shared by a team. Powerful words describe the unity of individuals working toward a common goal. Hopefully, your workplace team is healthy and overall operating with a positive vibe. However, I speak to many MSPs from across the country who have negative team experiences that are directly impacting their job satisfaction and will often resign their position.

Team culture does not only apply to professionals working within the same organization or the same department. Often, team culture transcends environments, organizations, departments, industries, countries, gender, social status, intelligence and ethnicity boundaries. As stated, teams are a group of individuals working toward a common purpose. These could include: community leaders, church committees, project teams, volunteer work in local or state professional organizations, MSPs representing multiple healthcare facilities working within a system and with an internal CVO, etc.

A good team culture can be a recruiting tool for new members because culture is created by the people composing the team – that is an exciting proposition! That is why the selection of people to a team is so important. Highly effective teams have a culture of collaboration, a willingness to share knowledge, to express themselves without fear of judgement,

106 ■ *The Executive Medical Services Professional*

an openness to ask questions, being respected and feeling supported.

Executives leading teams have a unique knack of inspiring others by creating an energy and enthusiasm among the team. This style motivates others to do the right thing in the best way possible to get the expected results. Highly effective leaders work to resolve differences quickly and directly. They, as well as their team members, thrive in collaborative environments. Another trait in promoting a healthy team culture includes leaders who support their members, encourage them to take risks and coach them to stretch their goals. Healthy teams practice ongoing and clear communication so all people on that team are kept informed. One of the most critical aspects in promoting a positive team culture is exhibiting and promoting trust. The lack of trust slows down everything and this phenomenon many times will negatively impact the professional as well as the personal lives of all involved. A high-performing team possessing a healthy team culture will approach and overcome challenges more easily. Be the leader who creates this positive experience for you and others. You all deserve to be a part of a healthy team!

Conversely, a toxic team culture is guided by the poor behaviors and decisions of the team. A dysfunctional culture just makes everything more difficult – from team relationships to their ability to accomplish goals.

12.4 Personal Beliefs

Your personal values are long-lasting beliefs about what is important to you. These beliefs become the core standards upon which people order their lives and make choices. A belief develops into a value when the person's commitment to it grows and they see it as being important. So, for example, my integrity and the respect I have for myself and others are my personal core values.

Facts Versus Perceptions, aka Leadership Blindness ■ **107**

Here's an example of what not to do as team member but especially as an organizational leader:

> The Medical Staff Services Department was located within the lobby of the Executive Suite at the hospital. A colleague and I were in ear shot of the hospital Administrator speaking to his Chief Operating Officer (COO) just outside my door and the COO asked the Administrator about his opinion of the Medical Staff Leaders. The Administrator responded, "These docs are arrogant and are always wanting something. They complain constantly and don't ever think about what is best for the hospital – only themselves. I really don't like too many of them."
>
> While listening to these Administrative representatives speak, I busied myself and acted very disinterested in their conversation. However, it took great control and emotional strength not to intercede when I heard such astounding words of judgement and disrespect expressed for the very professionals that bring patients into the hospital and with whom these Administrators collaborate daily. Although my behavior was calm and respectful on the outside, my mental voice was saying, "No this can't be true." I was so disheartened to learn that these Administrators felt this way and lacked any degree of sensitivity on what they said, how they said it, and that their words were so carelessly spoken.

There was definitely a clear lack of respect displayed in such a public way. Did I mention that these Administrators were also standing directly outside of the Doctors' Lounge? If these Administrators were willing to speak so thoughtlessly and publicly about physicians, it is safe to conclude that they obviously don't understand the importance of collaboration, respect. They also clearly lacked emotional intelligence. Relationships do matter!

108 ■ The Executive Medical Services Professional

Today, we live in a land of glass mirrors. Everything we say or do is available to others via recording, video etc. It is so important to think before we talk or act and to be able to quickly assess the consequences of our actions. We all have "off" days and say or do things we would not have done if we were not so distracted, tired or not feeling well. As an effective leader, you set the pace for others. My suggestion is this – if you are mentally, physically and/or emotionally exhausted – take a break, take a lunch outside the office, or simply take a mental health day (call it whatever is appropriate for you). If there is a critical meeting that requires your presence, ask for the meeting to either be postponed, or see if someone else can take your place. Self-care is an example of ensuring your professional habits and behaviors remain empowering, respectful and productive.

Georgia

QUESTIONS AND THOUGHTS TO GUIDE YOU

Do you fully understand the importance of effective leadership? Take time to look at the personal beliefs you bring to your organization. Are they healthy and appropriate? What positive examples from the department and team cultures could you find to complement, to encourage more of the same?

Next, you will learn how to influence leadership changes internally within the organization.

"When you change the way you see things, the things you look at change."
Wayne Dyer

Chapter 13

How to Influence Leadership Changes from Within

What It Takes to Get to the Top:
Working with a Higher Purpose for Everyone

Effective leadership can and does bring positive change to organizations. This change occurs when trust exists, when relationships are nurtured, and through consistent and thoughtful decision-making. As learned in previous chapters, the power, both positive or negative, of an organization, department or team lies within its culture. Culture must be respected but appropriately adjusted by leadership when situations arise. Effective leaders must also articulate a clear vision, take decisive action and get results through communicating expectations and accountability. When there is no leadership, toxic work environments are born.

110 ■ *The Executive Medical Services Professional*

13.1 Develop Managerial Effectiveness

Leadership is powerful where one person has the ability to influence or change the values, beliefs, behavior and attitudes of another person (Ganta, V.C. and Manukonda, J.K. (2014). Leadership During Change and Uncertainty in Organizations. *International Journal of Organizational Behaviour & Management Perspectives*, 3(3), 1183). Is that you?

Leaders are judged on how well they perform their work but also in how they lead and coach their teams. Successful project outcomes are no longer the only measurement of success for managers. Behaviors and consistently executed behaviors are markers for managerial success. Both successful outcomes and managing effective teams serve as lightning rods for advancement.

When you consider the traits of an effective leader, you recognize that these elements are essential when leading a team.

1. Experience: If you don't currently manage a team, volunteer to lead a project or a team.
2. Communication: Listening is as important as talking.
3. Knowledge: Identify your gaps and get busy.
4. Organization: The better organized, the greater perception of competence. Use your planner!
5. Time management: This is a must in being able to prioritize your day.
6. Reliability: You must deliver what you promise and always be available for your team. ALWAYS be on time!
7. Delegation: Let go and empower your team to do what they were hired to do.
8. Confidence: Be proud and inspire your team.
9. Respect for team members: The Golden Rule applies here. Be available, listen, be a resource and be kind.
10. Leadership: Lead with compassion and empathy. Give clear direction. Be decisive. Engage.

How to Influence Leadership Changes from Within ■ **111**

13.2 Inspire Others – Always

EMSPs inspire others through their natural style. If you need a little help in remembering how to connect and really motivate others to greatness, try these:

1. Care: Show people you care through your words and actions.
2. Be enthusiastic: Your genuine smile and positive energy will be contagious.
3. Trust: Show people that you are trustworthy. Can you keep a secret?
4. Stay positive: It's easy to jump on the band wagon of doubt and fear. Be the leader and find the sunshine through the rain.
5. Build others up: Find something good about someone else (it must be sincere) and make their day.
6. Admit your flaws: We are all human beings. Accept your shortcomings so others can relate to your vulnerability.
7. Actively listen: Truly comprehend what is being said. Make eye-contact, validate, ask questions and acknowledge understanding.
8. Reach for the stars: Dream big! Work your plan. Be ambitious. Never give up. You can accomplish anything!

You probably know at least someone in your life who has touched your heart in a way that remains special. Be that someone for someone else. Positive inspiration is powerful because it creates a sense of belief in someone that is stronger than themselves. You say it and they believe it and can then become better versions of themselves.

13.3 Develop Teams

As the healthcare industry continues to evolve, working within teams has become very important but working in effective

112 ■ *The Executive Medical Services Professional*

teams is essential. How can you make decisions that will create healthy and effective teams? The first factor you must consider when building a team – whether it is a team of employees or a project team – is that you must establish your leadership role with each team member. As you have already learned, this is done through trust, respect and consistent behaviors and not with your positional power.

Successful teams and their leaders demonstrate their effectiveness in the following ways:

1. Prioritizing work effectively
2. Sharing what's happening
3. Building a foundation of trust
4. Keeping goals visible and reinforcing them consistently
5. Pairing team members appropriately (looking for differences as well as similarities)
6. Running efficient meetings.

13.4 Leading Teams Through Change

You've probably heard the saying, "The only constant is change." Well that is true today, tomorrow and forever!

As effective EMSPs, you must be able to not only manage the changes that impact you and your work teams but actually thrive through change. This is definitely a skill that can be taught and mastered.

Here are just a few tips that will help in the transition of change. Remember, flexibility is the key to survival!

1. Keep your team informed of important details. Communicate! Communicate! Communicate!
2. Encourage your team to ask questions. In fact, set aside time for questions daily or weekly.

How to Influence Leadership Changes from Within ■ 113

3. Describe the planned change or changes that will impact the organization, your department and specifically the individual work being performed.
4. Roll out the change required of your team gradually (when possible) so they have time to adjust, clarify and perform.
5. Express appreciation for their work and positive attitude. Remember to celebrate your achievements!

13.5 Manage the Politics

Office politics is a reality. We all have a story or two to tell when office politics has worked against us and when it has worked in our favor. It has always been my position that when a situation arises that lacks logic – either in its etiology or resolution, that fear and greed are its drivers.

These fears are real and unfortunate for those on the receiving end of that fear. This can be based on their fear of looking incompetent, insecure, loss of respect, loss of control or power, etc. Fears can go as deep as the human psyche. That is why developing emotional intelligence (EI) skills as described in Chapter 10 is so important. In your leadership role, EI skills help you to understand why you react and respond in situations like you do. You can be more confident while maintaining your composure, as well as gaining greater insight into the behaviors and actions of others through compassionate understanding and accountability.

Office politics can be managed best by managing yourself with the keen skill of being able to transform a situation by changing how you receive and react to it.

You first want to ask yourself a few questions:

1. What am I afraid of?
2. What are he/she/they afraid of?
3. Are my fears realistic?

114 ■ *The Executive Medical Services Professional*

4. What is the bigger goal that I must work toward?
5. If this person was my friend, how would I respond?

The answers to these questions will help sort facts from fears. Then, you can have an informed conversation with those involved by stating the issue as objectively as possible, without placing blame. You will be able to seek their point of view. Remember, practice active listening skills and mutually agree on a resolution.

As leaders we have enormous power to influence others through our own attitude and intentions. It's important to try not to take things said or done too personally and to remind ourselves that we are all human. The leader who can be mindful about their behaviors and words during stressful situations has the greater power.

Look for examples of leaders who manage change effectively. Perform a Google search, watch videos, listen to podcasts, read about them or attend a live performance. One of the common traits I see in those who do this well is an understanding of politics, personalities and the power of negotiation. I regret not taking debate in school – I think this skill should be in everyone's toolbox. I didn't say this was easy – as so many in the military say, "the only easy day was yesterday".

Georgia

QUESTIONS AND THOUGHTS TO GUIDE YOU

What practices do effective leaders demonstrate? How do they set the pace for their teams? How do they connect and motivate those they lead? Today's strong leaders know and appreciate the fact that their teams' success depends on the examples they set, day in and day out.

How to Influence Leadership Changes from Within ■ **115**

Next, you will see some practical tips in effective leadership, noting the importance of practice and embracing your role as a leader.

"We will either find a way or make one."
Hannibal

Chapter 14

Coaching/Lessons in Leadership

What It Takes to Get to the Top:
Be the Leader Others Want to be Like

14.1 Tips from the Field as Shared by Others

Throughout my career as an EMSP and Executive Healthcare Administrator, I have learned from other very talented colleagues and administrative and Medical Staff leaders on the characteristics, behaviors and experiences that make a great leader.

Upon reflection of my own personal experiences, my consulting projects and my many thousands of conversations with other professionals, I've collected this list of leadership tips that summarize experiences lived and shared that reflect our successes. These lessons are brought to you as knowledge tips you can't live without!

1. Be kind
2. Be honest

118 ■ *The Executive Medical Services Professional*

3. Be respectful
4. Be competent
5. Be creative
6. Be confident
7. Be innovative
8. Be flexible
9. Be patient
10. Be resilient
11. Be open to receiving the word "no" as a challenge without taking it personally
12. Be wise in knowing when to quit a project, a job, a position or a career
13. Be a calculated risk taker
14. Be dependable
15. Be intuitive
16. Be compassionate
17. Be accountable and accept responsibility
18. Be a role model
19. Be physically and emotionally healthy
20. Be self-aware of emotions, thoughts and actions
21. Be a delegator
22. Be okay about saying no
23. Be dynamic
24. Be courageous
25. Be a believer in something greater than yourself
26. Be a skilled communicator
27. Be a great listener
28. Be an informed decision-maker
29. Be willing to learning something new
30. Be fabulous YOU!

14.2 Practice, Practice, Practice

As human beings none of us are perfect, so these industry leadership tips are yours to work on and to practice. Practice!

Coaching/Lessons in Leadership ■ **119**

Practice! Practice! Your honest effort will bring you rewards in demonstrating excellence, healthier relationships, stronger teams, more satisfying work environments and greater self-confidence. Trust yourself. You know what to do. The future is yours!

14.3 Embracing Your Role

An EMSP is a leader. Each of you must embrace the concept that leadership is part of you – regardless of your position title, to whom you report or your scope of work. You work to inspire, to produce quality, to be productive, to be good stewards of your resources, to use all available technologies in your work processes and practices, to work well with others by creating a culture of trust and by the ongoing encouragement of others.

Live boldly! Live passionately! Pursue your EMSP status as your journey to career success.

> I believe it is critical to look for those who have set the pace for others to follow. There are magnificent examples of leadership at its best. Think of someone you may know personally who has retired from an organization (and it does not have to be from the healthcare industry). Do a Google search and look for examples. Once you have your list compiled, then begin contacting them, either through a letter, email or telephone call. Have a short list of questions ready for them – you may be astounded at how willing they may be to share their knowledge. Yes, you will get some negative replies – expect it. I think you could get at least one short conversation out of ten attempts. You could ask the following:
>
> ■ What was the most painful management decision you had to make?
> ■ What was the most difficult negotiation you had to manage and why?

120 ■ *The Executive Medical Services Professional*

- What were three of the most rewarding experiences you had while holding your position?
- What, if anything, do you wish you had done differently?

You get the idea – I have done this many times over the course of my career and found the benefits to be immeasurable.

Georgia

QUESTIONS AND THOUGHTS TO GUIDE YOU

Use any of the qualities listed in this chapter, as well as others you select, and make a visual representation. Develop a list, in whatever order works for you, of the traits you admire in leaders. Then, put names from your personal and professional life with the traits. As you think about this, are there any traits that you admired many years ago, but do not feel are relevant today?

Do you see any that you would like to focus on to improve your leadership skills? If so, flag them for consideration. Then, take your document and put it in a suspense file for six months from now and review it again. You may be surprised at the results!

Next, you will read about the role of the servant leader. It is worth noting that many of the resources we have listed are written by and/or about servant leaders.

"Whatever you can do, or dream you can, begin it.
Boldness has genius, power and magic in it."
Johann Wolfgang Goethe

Chapter 15

Servant Leader

*What It Takes to Get to the Top:
Operate with Vision, Passion and Humility*

A servant leader, optimally, is one who serves first, builds trust, lives their values, listens to understand, adds value to others and demonstrates courage – thereby increasing their influence.

When I think of servant leadership, I automatically think of EMSPs representing the diverse Medical Staff Services industry. Many of you are working in organizations that consistently fail to recognize the value of the work performed either by inappropriate position titles, lack of recognition, poor position descriptions, low salaries or no leadership involvement. But, still, EMSPs demonstrate their commitment of servant leadership by serving first to protect the lives of patients through their fine-tuned credentialing practices. Most EMSPs that I have known over my 40+ year career are professionals who possess a servant's heart – you sincerely want to help others. This desire comes from a place of pure intent by not only identifying the needs but meeting the needs of your colleagues, stakeholders and others. You have a natural desire to promote

121

the well-being of those around you and have no reservations about championing a colleague on to success.

This sense of wellness – tapping into your passion of being a servant leader – flows forward into other areas of your life. Many leaders volunteer their services in professional, personal and social activities. This attitude of choice empowers teams, encourages others to perform at their highest potential and creates an environment of support and gratitude. Thank you for all you do. Pass it on!

15.1 Characteristics

A servant leader sets the organizational tone in several areas. They assemble a quality leadership team – building the functional disciplines (insightful, ethical, principled mindset), are skilled in their disciplines and are typically high achievers. They are collaborative, persuasive, and effective communicators. They are humble, with a clear understanding that they achieve success through the efforts of those who serve with and for them. They also conceptualize the future, with the ability to dream great dreams.

15.2 Approach to Organizational Issues

They create plans (roadmaps) for achievable results. They are careful to put people first, with genuine care and concern for those they serve. They have a clear understanding of those they serve, both directly and indirectly, and include stakeholders, both inside and outside the organization.

Servant leaders understand effective and efficient business strategies and, wherever possible, create cross-functional teams. They understand that how you get results is key to organizational success.

Servant Leader ■ **123**

They are careful to remember things their staff needs to hear them say: "You can; try it; I believe; how can I help; I'm sorry; that will not happen here; nice job."

Servant leaders believe in leadership versus authority; that leadership is not about them; that communication is a vehicle – not a scapegoat; and they develop a culture of accountability.

They commit to practice listening with empathy and awareness, which are critical to healing problems from words or actions within the organization.

With their foundation of strong emotional skills, character and vision, they tackle the issues most organizations have today – coping with high-tech issues, personnel (hiring, reviewing, firing etc.). They deal with sickness, layoffs, disability, alcoholism and substance abuse, sexual harassment and a host of other problems, as well as legal issues, always keeping the impact to groups as minimal as possible. Meaningful resolution many times requires courage and balance between the individuals involved.

Ken Blanchard and Phil Hodges, in their book *Servant Leader*, describe them this way:

> Servant leaders deal with and accomplish a mission with imperfect people. They recognize the need to establish a clear sense of purpose and direction. They recruit and select people to carry on the work. They do not avoid training, development and delegation issues. They understand the constant conflict demands on time, energy and resources. They resolve, where they can, turnover, betrayal and lack of understanding by friends and family. They take in stride constant scrutiny and challenges of commitment and integrity. Finally, they refuse to give into temptations of instant gratification, recognition and misuse of power.

124 ■ *The Executive Medical Services Professional*

Ultimately, servant leaders make other leaders stronger by the example they set and empower those around them to be the best they can be.

(Ken Blanchard and Phil Hodges, *Servant Leader*, Thomas Nelson, 2003, page 14 [excerpts from a list with the following question: Does Jesus have any relevant practical knowledge or experience in dealing with the following types of leadership issues I face day to day])

15.3 Executive Resources

Are there examples in your own organization of servant leaders? Where else do you see them operating? You might find it interesting to look at healthcare awards given to organizations by Malcolm Baldrige, the highest award that can be given to healthcare organizations for exceptional performance. Do you know any executives in other organizations who might be able to guide you? They do not have to be in your industry, they simply have to perform as a servant leader. You can carry out a Google search on servant leadership, and you will find a wealth of information. Another source of help in seeking information and guidance about being a mentor or strengthening your servant leadership skills is by searching the multitude of books available through Amazon.

Servant leaders are secure in their own skins. They are not arrogant, selfish, cruel, small-minded, jealous, pompous, uncaring, insensitive, judgmental, power-hungry, unfaithful, flippant, discriminatory, disrespectful, envious, undisciplined, negative or serial liars.

If you are fortunate enough to have worked with a true servant leader, think about what you liked most about them. Lastly, be grateful that you were able to watch, listen and learn from them.

Georgia

QUESTIONS AND THOUGHTS TO GUIDE YOU

Do you fully understand the importance of servant leadership? How many of the traits listed are those you exhibit? What steps could you take to improve your leadership style? This is not an easy path. If it were, there would be many more examples to follow.

Next, you will learn how to invest in your future, honestly assessing your financial circumstances, including family as collaborators and finding balance in both areas of your life.

"Competency goes beyond words. It's the leader's ability to say it, plan it, and do it in such a way that others know that you know how – and know that they want to follow you."
John C. Maxwell

Chapter 16

Invest in Your Future

What It Takes to Get to the Top:
Take Calculated Risks, Grow Through Action and
Never Stop Learning

Changes in healthcare and in business overall are occurring at a fast pace with more and more mergers and acquisitions being made to increase revenue or to even survive. Administrative decisions are being made all the time that potentially can impact your career and livelihood. EMSPs remain in control of their destiny by being in a "career ready" state. The healthcare term of survey readiness (being prepared for unplanned visits on an ongoing basis) was adapted specifically for this chapter because of the importance of being pro-active in your career planning by being career ready and always being prepared for the unknown implications affecting your position when decisions are made by others.

Not investing in yourself is like driving on a dead-end road without GPS to redirect you. You must be thoughtful and driven to develop a career plan that helps you achieve your career and life goals.

To assist you in reframing the importance of making your career a wise investment of your talent, believe the following:

128 ■ *The Executive Medical Services Professional*

1. Improving yourself can NEVER be a waste of time. It's the best investment you will make for your future success.
2. You are the President of your life and career. Believe in your power!
3. Your skills, emotional intelligence, networks and passion will drive your success.
4. You are talented.
5. You will accomplish your goals.
6. You can take risks to create your future.
7. You don't know everything so surround yourself with others who can help you.
8. Focus matters.
9. Having a positive attitude helps.
10. It's up to you!

If you are unsure how to begin developing your career plan, we can help with that! Visit www.teammedglobal.com or www.kamama.net.

People in corporate America used to be able to count on their organizations for financial support or at least time off to pursue education and training when planning for their professional future. Those days, for the most part, are gone. Company training is offered, but typically pointed toward specific organizational culture goals. Training for new technical innovation in a company would be a typical example.

However, after assessing your current areas of expertise and areas you will need for the future, you will probably see the need for training in more than one area. When you have identified these areas of needed competence (as identified earlier in Chapters 3 and 4), then it makes sense to see what resources you need to accomplish your education/training goals. Some will involve financial expenditures, such as Team Med Global University online interactive education and training program and some will be free via community courses, online programs, podcasts, workshops, webinars etc. It will probably take some time to make your assessments, then you

Invest in Your Future ■ **129**

will want to look at the bigger picture to include family collaboration and how to balance your professional and personal responsibilities.

16.1 Financial

Family budgets are usually tight to begin with – so how do you make room for yet one more commitment? This depends on several things – are there children, one person not working, acting as a caretaker, or an older parent living with you? What are the absolute essentials in the family budget (house payment, car payment, utilities, gas for cars, food, medical, childcare, children's sports, clothing) and what are some of the "nice to haves" (new cell phone, cable or satellite TV, eating out at least twice a week etc.).

If you do not have a detailed financial budget in place, whether on a computer or on paper, that is the first step to take. When you evaluate essentials, separated from "nice to haves", see what is left. At this point, you should also have looked at your professional development, education and training needs and wants, penciling in a dollar figure for this year and every year for the next five years. There are many options to consider. If the education is a high-dollar item and the household budget simply will not allow for it, there are long-term loans to evaluate, other forms of financial aid, personal loans and some people have simply used a GoFundMe account for part of their needs (gofundme.com).

16.2 Family Collaboration

When general information is ready, then it is wise to have a family meeting, involving all who are old enough to generally understand the issues. Children may need to make

130 ■ *The Executive Medical Services Professional*

a choice for only one extracurricular activity instead of several. Family vacations may need to be scaled back. Impulse buying may need to be curbed. Cars may need to be kept longer, as well as cell phones, computers and TVs. With small children, some bartering among friends may be necessary for you to spend extra time studying. A spouse may have to increase their household responsibilities so that you can concentrate on your education and training. Children may have to pick up more household chores (laundry, trash, meal preparation etc.). You may need to rearrange a room or part of one so that you can have space to study (family may need to clear the dinner table immediately so that you can use it for working). However, because the entire family is involved in your decisions, they are really a part of your success.

16.3 Finding Balance

Because you are adding additional responsibility to an already full plate, it is critical to have balance. With family or good friends in your area, you can and should set up a date night with your significant other at least once a month and have the children have a sleep over elsewhere. If older adults live with you, at the very least, have someone take them to dinner and a movie to give you and your spouse time alone – just for each other. If you are single and alone, get together with friends for a night out or have them come to your house for dinner and a movie on your big screen. You really need to build in simple rewards for the steps you are taking – none of this is easy or everyone would do it, right? The sacrifices you and others make are part of your setting up a positive future and the knowledge that you have shown the initiative and have persevered in the goals you have set for yourself. There may be a financial reward from work – a bigger raise, a promotion, or an opportunity to move to another organization where you have more upward

Invest in Your Future ■ **131**

mobility. Yet, the biggest reward is to and for you – helping you shape the future you want for yourself.

> One of the best gifts I think you can give yourself is letting go of things/people who no longer fit your needs. How many of you look at your phone before you even get out of bed – looking at email, social media etc.? How many outside organizations do you belong to that do not serve you? How many minutes of quiet time do you reserve for yourself every day? How many times do you go to the grocery store when you are hungry and spend more than you planned? How many times a week do you settle for fast food? Are your children committed after school every single day and many times on the weekend? For the record, I have done most of these things and more. When I began to realize that I was like a gerbil on a wheel and not serving myself or my family well, I began to slowly make changes, I resigned from all offices in professional organizations and from several of the organizations themselves. I began to more carefully plan my home menus and shop accordingly. I do not have social media on my cell phone – only on my computer. Fast food is now a luxury. I get up 15 minutes earlier to have quiet time before I do anything else. I am still working on balance, slowly making adjustments to the way I spend my time. If you do not begin, you will never get where you want to go.
>
> Georgia

QUESTIONS AND THOUGHTS TO GUIDE YOU

Have you done a deep dive to see what education and training you have completed over time? Have you listed all the education and training you believe you will need for the foreseeable future? Then, have you short-listed what

132 ■ *The Executive Medical Services Professional*

you will need for the next two to five years? Have you priced the training – everywhere from free to thousands of dollars? Then, armed with the information, are you meeting with your family to discuss budget matters? Remembering that balance is key, you will then want to take steps to make special time for your family, as they definitely will be impacted by your decisions.

Next, you will see how important affirmations and a sense of humor help to center you. Are you prepared to be a champion to others? An integral part of this trait is to motivate and inspire others, a powerful habit to form and practice.

> *"All you can change is yourself, but sometimes that changes everything!"*
> *Gary W. Goldstein*

Chapter 17

Things to Remember

What It Takes to Get to the Top:
Think and Be Positive, and Surround Yourself with Positive People

17.1 Affirmations – Why They Matter

What is your first thought when you hear the word "affirmation"? Please believe from our experience and to those whom we recommend the practice to – affirmations work!

Is this a technique that other people practice, and you have wondered if it is worth your time and energy to explore?

Dictionary.com says that an affirmation is the assertion that something exists or is true. Many successful leaders will tell you that, especially when they are down emotionally, physically or mentally, positive affirmations help build them back up and get them back on track. Affirmations come in all shapes and sizes, many from wisdom gained in the past. They are a guide to helping you visualize what you would like to do and/or become.

Today's work environments can be difficult to manage, even with improvements in technology and other areas of business. Stress, personality conflicts and frequently changing management take their toll on your disposition and view of the future.

133

134 ■ *The Executive Medical Services Professional*

What is your self-talk after a bad day at the office? How do you change your thoughts? You are responsible for yourself. While you can't typically change others' behavior, you can, over time and with practice, change your response. What can you do to create a positive outlook for yourself and set the example for others?

Learning to add affirmations to your daily routine may become one of your best kept leadership secrets. Think about affirmations beginning in your heart, traveling to your brain, and from there broadcasting to all your communication channels (hearing, speaking etc.). Who and what do you want to be and how are you going to get there? As you progress toward the executive level in your profession, you have both professional and personal challenges. Unless you have a special mentoring relationship with someone to help build and encourage you along the way, you are frankly on your own. You are personally going to have to find ways to build yourself up, every single day.

Affirmations can be used very effectively in every area of your life. They can help you to build confidence and self-esteem, improve relationships, point toward prosperity and abundance, improve physical, mental, emotional and spiritual health, motivate and encourage, and calm a variety of worries, leading toward peace and happiness. Most importantly, they should be used with a spirit of gratitude, becoming interwoven into the fabric of your career development.

In today's world, you can use any variety of mechanisms to help – your telephone, your computer, your iPad etc. Some use index cards, placing them in their wallet, in a desk drawer or taping them on a bathroom mirror at home. Some people memorize them and repeat to themselves often. If using a computer or laptop, they can be placed as an icon on your home screen. The point is that they need to be easily and routinely accessed.

Where do you find them? In today's world of instant communication, this is easier than it has ever been. Go to Team Med Global/Donna's social media posts of affirmations and

Things to Remember ■ **135**

motivation. She and Team Med Global were the first in the industry to push these daily energy blasts to help you start the day! Do a Google search, look for books, both online and in stores, take a few minutes in the card aisle at the grocery store and look for some, or look through your own personal book collection. Many people use Bible verses or mantras from older family members and friends. This is the easy part. Next, you need to sort through and see which ones "speak to you". Try them on – use one or two and if they do not work for you, try more until you see which ones fit you – where you are today, and where you want to be tomorrow. When do you use them? Our suggestion is to do this at least once daily, preferably twice – when you first get up and before you go to sleep at night. Leave a written copy on your bedside table – the best thing that can happen is for it to become smudged and worn until you must replace it.

How do you develop the habit? Schedule it like you would any other important event. You can put a daily reminder in Outlook, Google or any other application you happen to use. You can call it "affirmation time" or state the affirmation itself on the reminder. You will miss some – life will get in the way. When that happens, simply start again where you are right now. If you take a break or lunch during the day, try repeating the affirmation right before you go back to work.

The following are some ideas to get you started:

Gratitude Affirmations

- I am grateful to be alive today.
- I am grateful to be loved today.
- I am grateful to be a servant leader.
- I am grateful to be a life-long learner.
- I am grateful to be physically, mentally, emotionally and spiritually healthy.
- I am grateful to be able to help others.

136 ■ *The Executive Medical Services Professional*

- I am grateful for my troubles today. They will make me stronger and wiser tomorrow.
- I am grateful to be free.

Confidence/Self-Esteem Affirmations

- I grow more confident and stronger each day.
- I am the architect of my life. I design its structure.
- I build my life's foundation and choose its contents.
- I love myself and feel great about myself.
- I accept myself unconditionally.
- I like myself; I love myself; I am my very best friend.

Relationships and Love Affirmations

- My partner is coming into my life sooner than I expect.
- My heart is always open.
- I am surrounded by love.
- I love unconditionally and without hesitation.
- I am loved and appreciated by those around me.

Prosperity and Abundance Affirmations

- I am surrounded by abundance.
- I attract money effortlessly and easily.
- I continuously discover new avenues of income.
- I am open to all the wealth life has to offer.

Health Affirmations

- I am healthy, energetic and optimistic.
- Every day I get healthier and fitter.
- I care for my body by eating a healthy, well-balanced diet.
- I exercise regularly to strengthen my body.

Work and Career Affirmations

- My job adds satisfaction and fulfillment to my life.
- My career provides me the right opportunities to grow.
- I am valued and appreciated at my workplace.
- I perform my duties with the greatest diligence and attention.

Motivation/Encouragement Affirmations

- Every choice I make leads to bigger and better opportunities.
- I find something positive about every situation.
- I find optimistic ways of dealing with difficulties.
- I find ways to praise others and offer helpful suggestions.

Peace and Happiness Affirmations

- My most important goal is to be at peace, regardless of the situation.
- I make a conscious choice to be happy.
- My body is relaxed. My mind is calm. My soul is at peace.
- I feel joy and contentment in this moment.

Do not forget to reward yourself along the way. When you have practiced one or more affirmations for 90 days, treat yourself to something you would not usually do. Congratulations – keep it going!

17.2 Humor Helps

For the moment, let's put political correctness aside. There are really innumerable things we can find humor in – the antics of a puppy or kitten at play, the expression on a child's face when they taste something they like or don't, or when we put

138 ■ *The Executive Medical Services Professional*

something in a closet that belongs in the refrigerator – really, you haven't ever done that?

Experts have proven that laughter produces good endorphins, a positive feeling in the body. Today, aside from books and television, you have the internet and search engines to help you find things. Who has not looked at a YouTube video that has you nearly rolling on the floor and laughing until tears come into your eyes?

Think about some of the meetings you have been in where "grumpy" ruled the day and you left deflated and irritable. While you may not be able to change others' responses to issues, you can take steps to change your own. Try bookmarking a site that consistently has fun, humor-filled content. When you can, take five or ten minutes to watch it and let yourself relax.

What about the funny memories you have of when a new Administrator comes in and thinks he or she is doing something completely new and it is basically what you have been doing – your internal response is "here we go again". Think back of some of your travels to meetings or conferences. One I especially remember is standing in the TSA line, watching an adult with one-piece pajamas on (with a trap door) getting on the plane. Have you ever watched someone try to fit a bag that is too big into the overhead compartment, only to take it down and jump on it hoping to make it fit? – true story! Have we not "acromymed" ourselves to death – you know immediately when someone new hits a document with these and gets this glazed look on their face. What about credentialing stories? How many times have you looked at an application a doctor has submitted that is filled out correctly but attaches a picture of himself in a tuxedo and has cut the head off the person standing with him? Or the physician who has filled the forms out correctly assuming he will be put right on through – but fails the background check due to a criminal record.

17.3 Be a Champion to Others

Chapter 15 talks about mentoring relationships, which can be invaluable. An even deeper experience might be knowing someone is beginning work in a new area and offering to guide them by creating a project to help them learn the next steps in a monitored environment. Another approach might be to serve as an interview source for a 360 assessment. Would you be willing to serve as a guide for helping them with their professional development? Obviously, any of these need to be approached thoughtfully, keeping your own workload in mind. Yet, you know that one of the best learning tools for you is teaching someone else.

17.4 Motivate and Inspire as Only You Can Do

We all have gifts and each of us is unique. Looking at our strengths, we can and should offer our very best to the world. Using your talents, you can build others up; this is especially important when you can see someone is having a very bad day. You have seen bosses tear someone down, sometimes without their even realizing it. This is especially humiliating when done in public. Quietly observing a co-worker's body language and voice tone can give you a snapshot of their mood. You can then initiate a conversation that will brighten their day. It never hurts to have motivational tips displayed and even used at the bottom of emails. One organization even had a 90-day experiment of observing their employees and sending them a quick email every few days, recognizing their efforts and showing appreciation. The results were positive and far reaching.

140 ■ *The Executive Medical Services Professional*

Remember I mentioned earlier that I now get up 15 minutes earlier and set aside 15 minutes every morning for quiet time? Any day that this does not happen, my days seem more fragmented. I also now have this same practice at night. For those of you with children at home, you may have to lock yourself in the bathroom – but it is worth it! The world is filled with negativity and we simply must ignore it the best way we can and focus on the positives in life. One way I do this is to be careful about what I watch on TV or YouTube and refuse to read books that I know will upset me – no matter how well known the author is.

Georgia

QUESTIONS AND THOUGHTS TO GUIDE YOU

Where do you place affirmations so you can refer to them? How are you using humor to get you through the rough spots? Is there a situation where you could serve as a champion? How are you motivating and inspiring others? Remember that as an EMSP, you are the best of the best, setting the example as a healthcare leader and influencing the industry for the future.

Lastly, we will look at questions you need to answer to take charge of your future – to be the exceptional professional we know you can be.

"It's so important to know that you can choose to feel good. Most people don't think they have that choice."
Neil Simon

Chapter 18

Next Steps

You are in the driver's seat. By now, you should have a better idea of where you have been and where you are now. Your exciting future is frankly up to you.

- Do you want to remain where you are and doing what you are doing now? If not, what changes would you make to ensure the organization is aware of your value?
- Are you in a position to learn new skills, either where you are or in a different area of the organization?
- What personal changes in your resource management (home, family, friends, associates) are you willing to make to ensure you can make professional decisions that are in your best interest?
- Is your professional toolkit up to date? As part of this, do you have a copy of your position description and all performance reviews?
- Have you conducted your EMSP Competency Self-Assessment yet (Appendix I)?
- Have you evaluated available free and paid education and training programs to enhance your position? Have you

determined what changes you could make to your personal finance to obtain the information you need?

- Are you willing to take a lateral position to increase your competence?
- Are you willing to change jobs to get where you want to go?

Our fervent wish is your success! We have and will continue to build resources and programs that lead to your career success and personal wellness. Working together with you we can continue to make a difference. Stay tuned!

"You may be disappointed if you fail, but you are doomed if you don't try."
Beverly Sills

Appendix A

EMSP Professional Development Creed

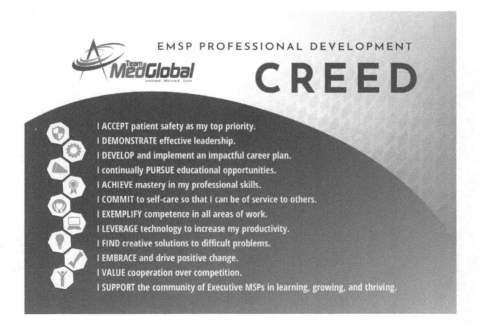

Appendix V

EMSP Professional
Development Events

Appendix B
EMSP Code of Conduct

EMSP CODE OF CONDUCT

EXECUTIVE MSPs ARE...

- Professionals with integrity
- Relentlessly innovative
- Committed to a safe work environment
- Creative and open-minded
- Willing to ask for guidance
- Proactive in voicing concerns
- Promptly responsive to work issues
- Accountable for mistakes
- Respectful and compassionate
- Actively involved in the EMSP community
- Mentors to others
- Passionate about work and life

Appendix C
EMSP Core Competency Formula

Appendix D

EMSP Core Competency Model

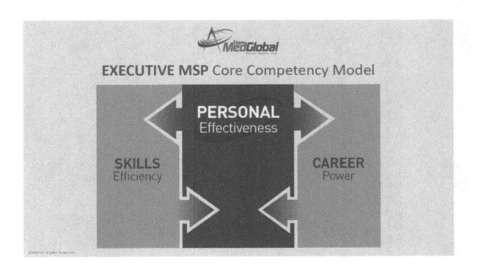

Appendix E

EMSP Value Assessment Tool

1. Abundance
2. Acceptance
3. Accessibility
4. Accomplishment
5. Accountability
6. Accuracy
7. Achievement
8. Acknowledgement
9. Activeness
10. Adaptability
11. Adoration
12. Adroitness
13. Advancement
14. Adventure
15. Affection
16. Affluence
17. Aggressiveness
18. Agility
19. Alertness
20. Altruism
21. Amazement
22. Ambition
23. Amusement
24. Anticipation
25. Appreciation
26. Approachability
27. Approval

28. Art
29. Articulacy
30. Artistry
31. Assertiveness
32. Assurance
33. Attentiveness
34. Attractiveness
35. Audacity
36. Availability
37. Awareness
38. Awe
39. Balance
40. Beauty
41. Being the best
42. Belonging
43. Benevolence
44. Bliss
45. Boldness
46. Bravery
47. Brilliance
48. Buoyancy
49. Calmness
50. Camaraderie
51. Candor
52. Capability
53. Care
54. Carefulness

55. Celebrity
56. Certainty
57. Challenge
58. Change
59. Charity
60. Charm
61. Chastity
62. Cheerfulness
63. Clarity
64. Cleanliness
65. Clear-mindedness
66. Cleverness
67. Closeness
68. Comfort
69. Commitment
70. Community
71. Compassion
72. Competence
73. Competition
74. Completion
75. Composure
76. Concentration
77. Confidence
78. Conformity
79. Congruency
80. Connection
81. Consciousness

82. Celebrity
83. Certainty
84. Challenge
85. Change
86. Charity
87. Charm
88. Chastity
89. Cheerfulness
90. Clarity
91. Cleanliness
92. Clear-mindedness
93. Cleverness
94. Closeness
95. Comfort
96. Commitment
97. Community
98. Compassion
99. Competence
100. Competition
101. Completion
102. Composure
103. Concentration
104. Confidence
105. Conformity
106. Congruency
107. Connection
108. Consciousness

EMSP Value Assessment Tool ■ **153**

109. Desire
110. Determination
111. Devotion
112. Devoutness
113. Dexterity
114. Dignity
115. Diligence
116. Direction
117. Directness
118. Discipline
119. Discovery
120. Discretion
121. Diversity
122. Dominance
123. Dreaming
124. Drive
125. Duty
126. Dynamism
127. Eagerness
128. Ease
129. Economy
130. Ecstasy
131. Education
132. Effectiveness
133. Efficiency
134. Elation
135. Elegance
136. Empathy
137. Encouragement
138. Endurance
139. Energy
140. Enjoyment
141. Entertainment
142. Enthusiasm
143. Environmentalism
144. Ethics
145. Euphoria
146. Excellence
147. Excitement
148. Exhilaration
149. Expectancy
150. Expediency
151. Experience
152. Expertise
153. Exploration
154. Expressiveness
155. Extravagance
156. Extroversion
157. Exuberance
158. Fairness
159. Faith
160. Fame
161. Family
162. Fascination
163. Fashion
164. Fearlessness
165. Ferocity
166. Fidelity
167. Fierceness
168. Financial independence
169. Firmness
170. Fitness
171. Flexibility
172. Flow
173. Fluency
174. Focus
175. Fortitude
176. Frankness
177. Freedom
178. Friendliness
179. Friendship
180. Frugality
181. Fun
182. Gallantry
183. Generosity
184. Gentility
185. Giving
186. Grace
187. Gratitude
188. Gregariousness
189. Growth
190. Guidance
191. Happiness
192. Harmony
193. Health
194. Heart
195. Helpfulness
196. Heroism
197. Holiness
198. Honesty
199. Honor
200. Hopefulness
201. Hospitality
202. Humility
203. Humor
204. Hygiene
205. Imagination
206. Impact
207. Impartiality
208. Independence
209. Individuality
210. Industry
211. Influence
212. Ingenuity
213. Inquisitiveness
214. Insightfulness
215. Inspiration
216. Integrity
217. Intellect
218. Intelligence
219. Intensity
220. Intimacy
221. Intrepidness
222. Introspection
223. Introversion
224. Intuition

154 ■ *The Executive Medical Services Professional*

225. Intuitiveness
226. Inventiveness
227. Investing
228. Involvement
229. Joy
230. Judiciousness
231. Justice
232. Keenness
233. Kindness
234. Knowledge
235. Leadership
236. Learning
237. Liberation
238. Liberty
239. Lightness
240. Liveliness
241. Logic
242. Longevity
243. Love
244. Loyalty
245. Majesty
246. Making a difference
247. Marriage
248. Mastery
249. Maturity
250. Meaning
251. Meekness
252. Mellowness
253. Meticulousness
254. Mindfulness
255. Modesty
256. Motivation
257. Mysteriousness
258. Nature
259. Neatness
260. Nerve
261. Nonconformity
262. Obedience
263. Open-mindedness
264. Openness
265. Optimism
266. Order
267. Organization
268. Originality
269. Outdoors
270. Outlandishness
271. Outrageousness
272. Partnership
273. Patience
274. Passion
275. Peace
276. Perceptiveness
277. Perfection
278. Perkiness
279. Perseverance
280. Persistence
281. Persuasiveness
282. Philanthropy
283. Piety
284. Playfulness
285. Pleasantness
286. Pleasure
287. Poise
288. Polish
289. Popularity
290. Potency
291. Power
292. Practicality
293. Pragmatism
294. Precision
295. Preparedness
296. Presence
297. Pride
298. Privacy
299. Proactivity
300. Professionalism
301. Prosperity
302. Prudence
303. Punctuality
304. Purity
305. Rationality
306. Realism
307. Reason
308. Reasonableness
309. Recognition
310. Recreation
311. Refinement
312. Reflection
313. Relaxation
314. Reliability
315. Relief
316. Religiousness
317. Reputation
318. Resilience
319. Resolution
320. Resolve
321. Resourcefulness
322. Respect
323. Responsibility
324. Rest
325. Restraint
326. Reverence
327. Richness
328. Rigor
329. Sacredness
330. Sacrifice
331. Sagacity
332. Saintliness
333. Sanguinity
334. Satisfaction
335. Science
336. Security
337. Self-control
338. Selflessness
339. Self-reliance
340. Self-respect

EMSP Value Assessment Tool ■ 155

341. Sensitivity
342. Sensuality
343. Serenity
344. Service
345. Sexiness
346. Sexuality
347. Sharing
348. Shrewdness
349. Significance
350. Silence
351. Silliness
352. Simplicity
353. Sincerity
354. Skillfulness
355. Solidarity
356. Solitude
357. Sophistication
358. Soundness
359. Speed
360. Spirit
361. Spirituality
362. Spontaneity
363. Spunk
364. Stability
365. Status
366. Stealth
367. Stillness
368. Strength
369. Structure

370. Success
371. Support
372. Supremacy
373. Surprise
374. Sympathy
375. Synergy
376. Teaching
377. Teamwork
378. Temperance
379. Thankfulness
380. Thoroughness
381. Thoughtfulness
382. Thrift
383. Tidiness
384. Timeliness
385. Traditionalism
386. Tranquility
387. Transcendence
388. Trust
389. Trustworthiness
390. Truth
391. Understanding
392. Unflappability
393. Uniqueness
394. Unity
395. Usefulness
396. Utility
397. Valor
398. Variety

399. Victory
400. Vigor
401. Virtue
402. Vision
403. Vitality
404. Vivacity
405. Volunteering
406. Warm-heartedness
407. Warmth
408. Watchfulness
409. Wealth
410. Willfulness
411. Willingness
412. Winning
413. Wisdom
414. Wittiness
415. Wonder
416. Worthiness
417. Youthfulness
418. Zeal

Questions and thoughts to guide you:

Have you evaluated your academic career?

This is important as many organizations are requiring degrees.

Do your skills and demonstrated personal effectiveness match the position you would like to have?

These components may well mean the difference between staying with your current job or having the job you really want.

Appendix F

EMSP Core Competency Model – Skills

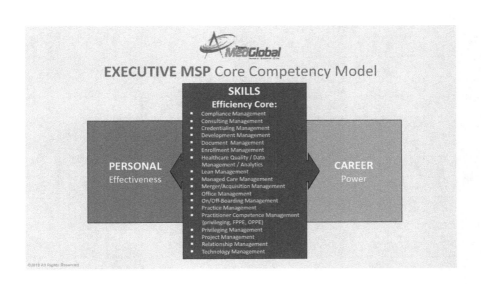

Appendix F

EMSP Core Competency Model – Skills

Appendix G

EMSP Core Competency Model – Personal

Appendix H
EMSP Core Competency Model – Career

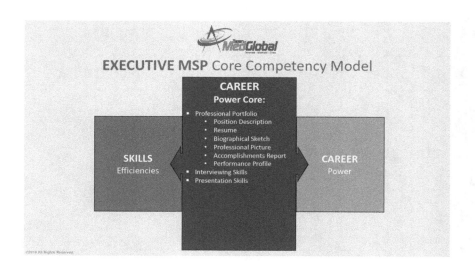

Appendix I

EMSP SELF-ASSESSMENT COMPETENCY TOOL

164 ▪ *The Executive Medical Services Professional*

EXECUTIVE MSP
SELF-ASSESSMENT COMPETENCY TOOL
M = Master C = Competent N = Needs Improvement I = Inexperienced

SKILLS DEVELOPMENT	PERSONAL DEVELOPMENT	CAREER DEVELOPMENT
____ Compliance Management	____ Analytical Thinking (Problem Solving)	____ Professional Portfolio
____ Consulting Management	____ Assertive Communication	____ Professional Picture
____ Credentialing Management	____ Centered Care/Wellness	____ Position Description
____ Development Management	____ Change Management	____ Resume
____ Document Management	____ Conflict Management	____ Biographical Sketch
____ Healthcare Quality Data Management/Analytics	____ Emotional Intelligence	____ Accomplishments Report
____ Lean Management	____ Influencing	____ Performance Profile
____ Managed Care Management	____ Innovation & Creative Thinking	____ Interviewing Skills
____ Merger/Acquisition Management	____ Negotiation	____ Presentation Skills
____ Office Management	____ Networking	
____ On/Off-Boarding Management	____ Self-Confidence	
____ Payer Enrollment Management	____ Stress Management	
____ Practice Management	____ Teamwork	
____ Practitioner Competence Management (privileging, FPPE, OPPE)	____ Time Management	
____ Privileging Management		
____ Project Management		
____ Relationship Management		
____ Technology Management		

Appendix J

EMSP Performance Profile

166 ■ *The Executive Medical Services Professional*

EXECUTIVE MSP PERFORMANCE PROFILE

Indicator	Goal Threshold: 75%	Plan	Performance Level	Recommendation
Technical/ Data Management	Improve database skills to: ■ Achieve "super user" level. ■ Develop training program for in-servicing department and medical staff. ■ Ensure optimal utilization of central database for medical staff operations and end users.	Seek outside training on database management from: ■ Internal IT training programs. ■ MSP Tech Squad. ■ Vendor training programs. ■ Local junior college adult education programs.	60% Needs Improvement	Conduct gap analysis of technical improvement areas within 90 days. Determine resource available to improve technical skills to "expert" level. Utilize new knowledge to create training programs for: ■ Internal stakeholders ■ External stakeholders
Electronic Delivery/ Meeting Management	Improve turnaround times for meeting materials. Transition meeting materials from hard copy to paperless.	Prepare and distribute meeting information to committee members within 30 days of meeting date. Incorporate meeting materials into an electronic format for meeting presentation.	100% Excellent	Establish standing appointments for committee/ department chair review and electronic sign-off of meeting information prior to distribution and meeting. Obtain support from President of Staff on the use of electronic delivery of meetings and resources.

				Create live stream, Power-Point and hardcopy training materials to in-service chairs on automation features.
Department Availability/ Staffing Management	Realign department hours of operation to increase staff availability to medical staff.	Decrease staff "tardiness" by 100% by transitioning to expanded hours and staggered scheduling that meet both staff and medical staff needs.	75% Needs Improvement	Expand department hours from 7 am to 6 pm by staggering staff hours. Inform medical staff of expanded department hours through newsletter, electronic display board, website and meeting agendas.
Onboarding: Committee Members Department Staff	Decrease meeting times and completion of actions due to lack of new member understanding of processes. Decrease department work product turn-around times and staff overtime		50% Needs Improvement	Create annual on/off-boarding program for MS Committees and Board. Create onboarding program for new department staff members to incorporate all internal/external customer functions and expectations. Develop department annual staff training to review changes in:

(Continued)

(Cont.)

Indicator	Goal Threshold: 75%	Plan	Performance Level	Recommendation
				■ Company mission/vision ■ Regulatory/accreditation ■ Requirements ■ Internal policy/procedure
Compliance Management	Develop compliance integration plan for internal/external customers to guarantee "survey ready" status.	Identify internal/external customers. Identify compliance needs for both internal/external customers. Develop standardized tools per customer compliance needs to retain "survey ready" status. Training of customers on compliance requirements. Implementation of rotating "mock survey" to avoid "crisis" survey preparations.	100% Excellent	Continue with current plan.

Professional Development	Incorporate professional development expectations and requirements into: ■ Monthly staff meetings ■ Onboarding ■ Annual training	Conduct gap analysis of training needs to include MSP Core Competencies (see model).	80%	Research internal and external sources (EMSP Program) for professional development specific to staff needs. Determine budgetary needs for department professional development, to include certifications in medical staff services and quality management. Develop cross-training program among internal staff.
Personal Development	Improve relationships with internal and external stakeholders by gaining information and tools on emotional intelligence and time management. Develop healthy work/life balance by utilizing tools available to implement self-care practices. Reduce stress by better time management skills and eliminate "crisis" mode mentality.		90%	Enroll and participate in programs for emotional intelligence and time management within 180 days. Seek outside online courses (EMSP Program) and other programs and hard copy materials focused on improvement of emotional intelligence and offering usable tools for managing personal/professional time effectively and efficiently.

Appendix K

EMSP Position Statement

EXECUTIVE MSP POSITION STATEMENT

VALUE MESSAGING

■ Must Be:

☐ Clear
☐ Compelling
☐ Relevant to Listener
☐ Created/Modified to Fit the Situation

■ How Does It Work?
■ Two Steps:

☐ Step 1: "Do you know how _____?"
☐ Step 2: "Well what I do is _____."

MY FORMAL EMSP POSITION STATEMENT:

_____
_____
_____
_____
_____
_____

■ Examples: **WEAK**

☐ "I work as a Medical Staff Services Professional."
☐ "I credential doctors."
☐ "I'm responsible for managing all the activities that pertain to the providers in our health plan."

■ Examples: **STRONG**

☐ "Do you know when you have a loved one in the hospital and you want to know that only qualified doctors are taking care of them"?

"Well, that's what my department does. We investigate the background of doctors to make sure that only the most qualified are allowed to practice."

☐ "Do you know how important it is that a doctor's qualifications are investigated"?

"Well, what I do is lead my team to verify that the physician's training, education and experience are accurate and valid."

☐ "I'm like the Doctor FBI."

Appendix L

Reference Guides

Alain, Patrick. *The Leader Phrase Book*: Rupa Publications, 2012.

Anca, Andrei. *Lead from Any Seat*: Andrei Anca, 2019.

Bates, Suzanne. *All The Leader You Can Be: The Science of Achieving Extraordinary Executive Presence*: New York: McGraw-Hill Education, 2016.

Bennis, Warren. *Managing the Dream – Reflections on Leadership and Change*: Harper Collins Publishers, 2000.

Bradberry, Travis and Greaves, Jean. *Emotional Intelligence 2.0*: TalentSmart, 2009.

Brown, Brene. *Braving the Wilderness: The Quest for True Belonging and the Courage to Stand Alone*: New York: Random House, 2017.

Canfield, Jack. *The Success Principles – How to Get from Where You Are to Where You Want to Be*: New York: Harper Collins Publishers, 2005.

Clear, James. *Atomic Habits: An Easy & Proven Way to Build Good Habits & Break Bad Ones*: New York: Penguin Random House LLC, 2018.

Dumas, John Lee. *The Mastery Journal: Master Productivity, Discipline and Focus in 100 Days*: John Lee Dumas, 2017.

Dumas, John Lee. *The Freedom Journal: Accomplish Your Goal in 100 Days*: John Lee Dumas, 2015.

Goestenkors, Donna and Day, Georgia. *The Medical Services Professional Career Guidebook*: CRC Press, 2012.

174 ■ *The Executive Medical Services Professional*

Hyatt, Michael. *Platform: Get Noticed in a Noisy World: A Step-by-Step Guide for Anyone with Something to Say or Sell*: Nashville, Tennessee: Thomas Nelson, Inc., 2012.

Hyatt, Michael. *Your Best Year Ever: A 5-Step Plan for Achieving Your Most Important Goals*: Grand Rapids, Michigan; Baker Books, 2018.

Macdonald, Mac Alexander and Lyfe Enhancement Company. *Lighting Your Own Fuse: A Glossary of Mission, Vision and Passion*: Rory Briski and Deborah Drake Productions Consultants, 2014.

Miller, Donald. *Building a Story Brand: Clarify Your Message so Customers Will Listen*: New York: Harper Collins, 2017.

Niven, David PhD. *The 100 Simple Secrets of Happy People: What Scientists Have Learned and How You Can Use It*: New York: Harper Collins, 2001.

Robbins, Mel. *The 5 Second Rule: Transform Your Life, Work, and Confidence with Everyday Courage*: United States of America: Savio Rebvblic, 2017.

Russell, Lou. *10 Steps to Successful Project Management*: Lou Russell, 2007.

Schwarz, Joyce. *The Vision Board – The Secret to an Extraordinary Life*: Collins Design and Joyce Schwartz: New York, 2008.

Tuhovsky, Ian. *Communication Skills Training*: Ian Tuhovsky, 2017.

Index

2008 financial crash 68

A

ability 18
abundance affirmations 136
academic assessment 16–17
acceptability of interactions 104
Acquired Immune Deficiency
      Syndrome (AIDS) 61
actions taken in organizational
      culture 38
adaptability 54
adaptation 31–42
adequacy 9
administrative roles
      1–2, 77, 89–90
affirmations 133–137
Angelou, M. 92
area of specialty principles 52–53
assessment
    academic 16–17
    personal effectiveness needs
        20–28
    of self 21–22, 34
    skills 15
    workplace 17–20
awareness 1–8, 84–85, 86–88

B

Baby Boomers 57, 58–60, 62–63, 64
balance, finding 130–131
behaviors 101–102, 104
Bennett, R.T. 81
Blanchard, K. 123–124
Brajdic, A. 105
Business in Context
    An Introduction to Business and
        Its Environment (Needle)
        101–102

C

capacity 9
careers 10–11
    adaptation/growth 31–34
    affirmations 137
    future 10–11
    portfolios 46, 47
    power competencies 19–20,
        36–37
    readiness 46
champion mindsets 139
change
    embracing of 104
    influence/self-awareness 109–115

176 ■ *Index*

character 93–99
Chief Executive Officers (CEOs) 75,
    85–86
Chief Operating Officers (COOs) 107
Churchill, W. 7
coaching/lessons in leadership
    117–120
Code of Conduct 4, *5*
communication
    emotional intelligence 84
    generational shifts 63, 64
    position statements 52–53
    transferrable skills 54
compassion 83–89
competencies 9–13
    adaptation/growth 31–42
    emotional intelligence 83–91
    formula 18–19, 37–38
    industry specialties 51–54
    professional development 9–10
    Self-Assessment Tool 34
    workplace assessment 17–20, *19*
competition 76
confidence 51–56
    affirmations 136
COOs *see* Chief Operating Officers
core competencies
    emotional intelligence 83–91
    strengths/weaknesses 43–44
    workplace assessment 17–20, *19*;
        see also competencies
crash of 2008 68
credentialing 44–45
Credentials Verification Organization
    (CVO) 44–45, 52–53, 72
culture
    evaluation 34–37
    leadership blindness 101–105
    organizational 37–41
    team culture 105–106
customer service 38
customized competency models
    51–54

D

decision-making 38, 94, 95
Denworth, L. 88
department culture 103–105
dependability 54
dictionaries 9, 93
digital knowledge 61
Disney, W. 65
Disraeli, B. 99
doctors 67–68
Duval, S. 86
Dyer, W. 108

E

education and training programs
    128–129
effectiveness/efficiency 19–20,
    32, 35–36; *see also*
        competencies
EHA *see* Executive Healthcare
    Administrator
elevator pitches 52–53
emotional intelligence (EI) 83–92
    leadership blindness 103
    politics management 113
    relationship management 84–85,
        88–89
    self-awareness 84–85, 86–87
    self-management 87
    social awareness 87–88
empathy 83–89
employee satisfaction 39–40,
    104–105
encouragement affirmations 137
engagement 64
enrollment 52–53
    software 44–45
equality between genders
    68–70
ethics 94
European Union (EU) 59

Executive Healthcare Administrator
(EHA) 1–2
Executive MSP – Value Assessment
22–28
executive resources 124
external stakeholders 96–97

F

family collaboration 129–130
feedback 22–28
financial crises 68
financial investments 129
flexibility 15–29
formula 18–19, 37–38
future
careers 10–11
investment in 127–132

G

Ganta, V.C. 110
gender roles 67–73
equality 68–70
needs/wants 70–72
stereotypes 67–68
generational shifts 57–65
differences/similarities 58–62
Generation Jones 58, 59–60
Generation X 57, 58, 60–61,
62–63, 64
Generation Y 57, 58, 61–63, 64
Generation Z 57, 58, 62
implications 62–64
Millennials 57, 58, 61–63, 64
types 58
Goestenkors, D. 6–7
Goethe, J.W. 120
Goldstein, G.W. 132
Goleman, D. 84, 88
"The Good and Bad of Empathy" 88
good character 93–99

Gotham Culture 101
gratitude affirmations 135–136
growth 31–42

H

habits/behaviors 101–102, 104
happiness 39–40, 104–105
affirmations 137
Hay Group 63
health affirmations 136
Healthcare Consultants (HCs) 52–53
healthy teams 39–40, 104–105,
106, 137
high performing EMSPs 64, 90
highly functioning EMSP 78
Hodges, P. 123–124
holidays 85–86
honesty 94
Human Immunodeficiency Virus
(HIV) 61
Human Resources
academic assessment 16
gender roles 72–73
strengths/weaknesses 48
humor 137–138

I

industry specialties 51–54
influence/inspiration
109–115, 139
integrity 94
internal stakeholders 96–97
investing in the future 127–132
isolated MSP 78

J

Jones, Generation 57, 58, 59–60
Jordan, M. 13
July 4th holiday 85–86

K

keeping up with the Joneses 58, 59–60
Keller, H. 73
knowledge 18, 61

L

leadership
    attributes 77–80
    blindness 101–108
    coaching/lessons 117–120
    culture evaluation 34–37
    generational shifts 63
    inner change 109–115
    organizational culture 38–39
    rethinking 75–81
    servant leaders 121–125
    strengths/weaknesses 46–47
    traditional vs. transformational 75–76
    traits 77–80
    transferrable skills 54
Leadership During Change and Uncertainty in Organizations (Ganta & Manukonda) 110
letters of resignation 97–98
Locums Tenens (LT) 52–53
love affirmations 136
loyalty 63

M

Managed Care Organization (MCO) 52–53
management
    emotional intelligence 84–85, 87, 88–89
    gender roles 70–71
    generational shifts 64
    politics 113–114
    quality managers 46–47
    of self 84–85, 87
    technology 54
Manukonda, J.K. 110
Marston, R. 29
Maxwell, J.C. 125
The Medical Services Professional Career Guidebook – Charting a Development Plan for Success 46
Medical Staff Services Department (MSSD) 44–45, 52–53
    academic assessment 16
    gender roles 71, 72–73
    leadership blindness 107
    servant leaders 121
mediocre performances 2–3
micromanagement 88–89
Millennials 57, 58, 61–63, 64
moral strength 94, 95
motivation 64, 139
    affirmations 137
mutual respect 38

N

NAMSS 6–7
national holidays 85–86
Needle, D. 101–102
needs assessment 20–28, 44–45
negative thoughts 45, 106
The New American College Dictionary 9
North Atlantic Treaty Organization (NATO) 59

O

online interactive education and training programs 128–129
organization, transferrable skills 54

Index ■ 179

organizational culture 37–41,
101–103
organizational issues 122–124

P

past impact (backgrounds) 10–12
Pavlina, S. 22
payer enrollment 44–45,
52–53
peace affirmations 137
personal beliefs 106–107
personal competencies 19–20
adaptation/growth 31–34
leadership culture evaluation
35, 36
needs assessment 20–28
Pew Research Center 57–65
politics 113–114
Pontell, J. 58–60
portfolios 46, 47
position statements 52–53
positivity 133–137
power competencies 19–20, *33*,
36–37
power of words 53–54
Practice Management (PM) 52–53
Presidents of an organization 75
professional development
competencies 9–10
professional performance profiles
46, 47
project managers 70–71
prosperity affirmations 136
purchasing needs assessment
44–45

Q

quality managers 46–47
quality of service 38
quality work products 104

R

recognized EMSP Specialties 52
redesigning of department
operations 44–45
relationship
affirmations 136
management 84–85, 88–89
replacing needs assessment 44–45
resignation 97–98
respect 38, 83–89
roadmaps (organizational issues) 122
Robbins, T. 56
Roget's II The New Thesaurus 93

S

satisfaction 39–40,
104–105
Scientific American 88
self-assessments 21–22, 34
self-awareness 84–85, 86–87,
109–115
self-confidence 51–56
self-esteem affirmations 136
self-improvement 9–13
self-management 84–85, 87
self-talk 133–137
Servant Leader (Blanchard &
Hodges) 123–124
servant leaders 121–126
sexually transmitted disease 61
shaping of culture 104
Sills, B. 142
Simon, N. 140
skills competencies 10
adaptation/growth 31–34
assessment 15
core competencies 18
efficiency 19–20, 35–36
leadership culture evaluation 35
social awareness 84–85, 87–88

180 ■ *Index*

social independence 67–68
social media 6
software 44–45
staff turnover 39
stakeholders 96–97
stereotypes 67–68
strengths/weaknesses 43–49,
94, 95
success 46, 51–56, 78
sufficiency 9

T

team culture 105–106
team development 111–112
Team Med Global (TMG) 18,
128–129, 134–135
teamwork 54
technology 54, 68
Temporary Staffing (TS) 52–53
A Theory of Objective Self Awareness
(Duval & Wicklund) 86
toxic team culture 106
Tracy, B. 42
traditional gender roles 69–70

transferrable skills 54–56
truth 94
turnover of staff 39

U

upgrading needs assessment
44–45

V

value of character 96–98

W

Walt Disney 65
weaknesses and strengths 43–49
Wicklund, R. 86
work affirmations 137
work–life balance 6
workplace assessment 17–20

Z

Ziglar, Z. 49